Provoking the Gospel

Provoking
the Gospel

METHODS TO EMBODY
BIBLICAL STORYTELLING
THROUGH DRAMA

Richard W. Swanson

THE PILGRIM PRESS   CLEVELAND

for my teacher
Donald H. Juel

The Pilgrim Press, 700 Prospect Avenue, Cleveland, Ohio, 44115-1100
www.pilgrimpress.com
© 2004 by Richard W. Swanson

All rights reserved. Published 2004
Printed in the United States of America on acid-free paper

09   08   07   06   05   04   5   4   3   2   1

Library of Congress Cataloging-in-Publication Data

Swanson, Richard W., 1952–
    Provoking the gospel : methods to embody biblical storytelling through
drama / Richard W. Swanson.
        p. cm.
    Includes bibliographical references.
    ISBN 0-8298-1573-2 (pbk. : alk. paper)
    1. Bible stories.   2. Storytelling—Religious aspects—Christianity.
3. Bible plays.   4. Drama in Christian education.   I. Title.

BS546.S88 2004
246'.72—dc22

                                                            2004044396

CONTENTS

PREFACE

This book grows out of the conviction that biblical stories are public stories. These old stories come out of painful and complicated worlds and represent valiant attempts to engage that pain and complication, to wrestle with it rather than retreat from it. They are stories of public resistance and need to be read as such if they are to be read responsibly.

Proper biblical interpretation is not done *for* the church alone, *by* the church alone, and *in* the church alone. Rather, interpretation is and must be a public act, and that means that insiders who tell these stories publicly should expect to be changed by that act and by their audiences. If these old stories are well and properly told, those audiences will include both insiders to the stories and outsiders. If these stories are well and properly told, they will draw a public audience simply because the stories are good. But if these old stories are public stories in that particularly demanding sense of the word, then it follows that these texts are not mere tools in the ideological control of the church. As both script and scripture, these stories have their own power and integrity. But such power and integrity are truly encountered when the stories are taken seriously in public performance. Public performance cannot expect to succeed because of some kind of ideological special pleading. Public performance must avoid what Shimon Levy calls the "mutually complementary 'kitsch or pathos' syndrome, so typical to holy shows."[1] Instead, public performance must accept the risk of being changed both by the text and by the audience.

This book grows also out of the conviction that biblical stories are physical stories. Because biblical stories come out of real life, and because real life is unrepentantly physical, real interpretation of these old stories must be physical to be responsible.

As a consequence, this book argues that biblical interpretation must concern itself first of all with bodies, not ideas. The characters in these stories are not symbolic ciphers; they are bodies, they are people, and their interactions take place in the physical and ethical space of the real world. This ethical space is crucial. In biblical stories people look each other in the eye and act. These acts sometimes heal and sometimes betray, sometimes protect and sometimes abuse. This is the way it is with *all* human activity in the real physical and ethical space of the world. So public performance of these physical stories will draw its (sometimes surprising) life from contemporary acts of healing and betrayal, protection and abuse.

This book grows, finally, out of a commitment to what I call "provoking the gospel." Contentment with the same old readings of biblical stories leads to *rigor mortis.* We need to poke these old stories, to poke them and provoke them a little. And nothing does that textual poking and provoking like public, physical performance. If you can continue to pretend that these old stories are calm compilations of ideas (*our* ideas!), then "same old" readings will be fine. But public audiences will not sit still for dull, formulaic performances. So if we dare to accept the risk and challenge of playing these fascinating old stories for audiences who are free to see what is actually there, free to react, respond, and argue, then we will need to learn how to poke hard at these stories.

We ought also to expect these old stories to poke us back, to provoke us (and the audience) sometimes in ways we had not expected and do not like. These stories, after all, are not house pets. They are wild and free, and some of the best ones cannot ever be housebroken. The story of Abraham's willingness to kill his son (Genesis 22) is a savage story, and putting a bow around its neck will not change that fact. Such a text will provoke anyone who tries to play it honestly in front of an audience that can see the faces of both Abraham and his son, his only son, Isaac, whom he loves.[2]

This book expects, most important of all, that the process of provoking the gospel will, in fact, call the gospel out of these old stories, these texts, these scripts that are scripture. This book expects, further, that these old stories provide (as they always have provided) a powerful occasion to call the gospel out in the midst of the players and the audience. These old stories, if they are properly provoked as public, physical texts, provoke the gospel out of both audience and players in ways that will continue to surprise, now as through their whole history. This book expects that it is only through this risk that God speaks life into a world in love with death. As Salman Rushdie wrote in his essay "Imaginary Homelands," "I must say first of all that description is itself a political act. . . . So it is clear that redescribing a world is the necessary first step towards changing it. . . . So literature can, and perhaps must, give the lie to official facts."

This book grew out of my work as a preacher in rural Wisconsin, out of my work as a professor at Augustana College, and out of six years of work on the *Provoking the Gospel Project,* a collaborative venture involving (now) a multigenerational team of storytellers. From its first trial as a teaching tool, through the early experiments with my pioneering team of storytellers, through workshops and performances, resistant students and receptive ones, this way of working with biblical stories has drawn me deeper and deeper into an exploration of a surprisingly powerful interpretive method. I hope in this book to draw you also into something that has completely changed the way I work with the Bible.

This work has been collaborative from the start. Performance always is, because even in a one-person show the audience is a creative partner. But that means that there are more debts involved in this work than I can easily note. I must thank my initial team of storytellers: Melissa Larsen, Erika Iverson, Michael T. Smith. We met and worked and hunted for something we could smell, but not see. They have been marvelous hunting partners. That pioneering team has now been expanded to include many others: Brooke Baker, Kristin Barnett, Kira Christensen, Jason Dybsetter, Katie Fick, Jennie Graves, Amanda Mitchell, Desiré Kelly,

Kerri Smith, Meghan Swanson, Mandy Youngers, Kristin Zingler. It was in working with these talented and generous people that I discovered how large this project was, and how promising. As I watched them, a collection of various kinds of insiders and outsiders, develop into a team that works nimbly, creatively, and ferociously with biblical texts, I realized that this book had to be written. I have learned more from them than I can say. Everyone should get a chance to work with and learn from such a team.

I would like also to thank Augustana College for providing me with a sabbatical leave that allowed this project to begin. I'd like to thank the trustees of the Granskou Award, the South Dakota Synod of the ELCA, and the trustees of the Clara Lea Olson Endowment. Each of these groups provided funding and encouragement as the project has developed. Special thanks goes also to the members of the Theatre Department at Augustana College: Ivan Fuller, Julia Pachoud, and Michael Reese. They have been more than generous in allowing me to use their space and their considerable technical expertise as I have worked on this project.

Such work is not possible without the sharp eyes and perceptive critique shared by colleagues and friends, especially Murray Haar, Sandra Looney, and Vicki Fuller at Augustana. Special thanks to Tom Boomershine, David Rhoads, Dennis Dewey, Robert Fowler, Elizabeth Struthers-Malbon, Joanna Dewey, Whitney Shiner, and Amy-Jill Levine, colleagues who have been a gift from God. They have viewed this project in various stages of its development and have generously provided vital critique and encouragement.

And I would like to thank my students, especially those who heard in these old stories something that comforted and challenged them, provoked them and gave them life, and thus taught me why this work matters.

Above all, I would like to thank my teacher, Donald Juel. Years ago I walked into his office wanting to study the gospel of Mark. I came equipped with my prospectus, my bibliographies, my plan of action. He reminded me that I perhaps ought to read Mark's story before I did anything else. Out of this simple suggestion have come twenty years of productive work with biblical narrative. More important: out of this simple encounter came twenty years of work with a teacher and scholar and fellow worker, a gracious, generous, and provocative man who, again and again, called the gospel out of his many students. I am grateful to have been one of that group. From him I learned my first lessons in provoking the gospel, and it is to him and to his memory that this project and this book are dedicated.

INTRODUCTION
It's Not Just Bible Stories Anymore

This is a "how-to" book about storytelling.

Simple enough. There are other such books, and like them, this book has suggestions, exercises, and examples that will help get you started telling biblical stories.

What makes this book different is that it is also a "why-to" book.

This is not such a simple matter. Maybe it should be simple. On the one hand, the narrative texts in the Bible come out of oral tradition. That should be a simple enough reason for exploring them orally, and it is. On the other hand, those of us who come out of a background of attending Sunday school may very well have a strong acquaintance (for good or ill) with biblical storytelling. If it's already being done in every little church on the planet, why read (or write!) a "why-to" book about it? Good question.

But on the other hand (I find that decent thought requires at least three hands, sometimes more), the kind of biblical storytelling I am talking about is sufficiently different, sufficiently surprising, and sufficiently powerful to provide a whole new "why" for biblical storytelling.

This is a "why-to" book about exploratory ensemble biblical story-telling: storytelling done by a team, storytelling that is experimental. More about that later.

Why do it this way?

For many years I have been teaching courses that include exploration of the creation stories in Genesis 1 and 2. These stories, interesting enough on their own, become far more interesting when you investigate not only the stories themselves but also the social and historical context out of which they come. These stories were first told, at least in the form we now have, by the Jewish community in exile, by the people who had been conquered by the Babylonians, ripped from their homes, and hauled into captivity in Babylon. But these stories become positively fascinating when they are read next to and compared with the creation story that was told in Babylon in those days. It's one thing to know that the Jewish community in exile told these stories in order to keep their memory and tradition alive; it's quite another to see the ways the stories in Genesis 1 and 2 have been shaped to block and modify the Babylonian story.

In my years of teaching with these stories, I have found ways to help students see this blocking and modifying. It has usually worked, more or less. Students always saw that the Jewish community tried to resist outside influence, and usually understood that this resistance was a survival tactic. Some students, however, saw in the tactic a justification for resisting any new idea. Of these students, some rejected such resistance while others heartily embraced it. This made for a strange mix in the classroom. It also led to a tendency to misunderstand biblical narrative and biblical interpretation.

And then I changed the way I presented the material. For years I have had my students read the Marduk and Tiamat story out of Enuma Elish, the Babylonian creation epic. For years I have told them this story myself. This proved more effective than silent reading, but remained limited. Students recognized that the story was different, surprising, and that it possessed its own integrity. Those who equated novelty with danger rejected it out of hand. Those inclined to be more hospitable found aspects of the story that they liked and disliked. Sometimes they noticed the presence of a female deity, and sometimes they noticed her strength, and even liked it.

Then I changed the way they engaged this story. Instead of having them read the story, or simply telling it to them, I brought in a colleague, a skilled actor, to play the part of Marduk opposite to Tiamat, played by a young woman in the class, also a skilled actor.

They played the scene. Tiamat's legs "shook to the roots, both together." Marduk entrapped her and "extinguished her life." These elements had always been part of the story, but suddenly the story was different. What had seemed safe and mythic was suddenly a story about women and men, about one woman and one man, and about the violence that too often shatters that relationship.[1]

The effect on the class was stunning. The task of the class from the start had been to develop a way to tell the creation stories that was instructive and compelling. No longer was this an "academic exercise" to be finished and forgotten. Suddenly the telling of an effective counter-story was physically necessary. Suddenly the students knew why the Jewish community in exile had also found it physically necessary to tell an effective counter-story. Suddenly they comprehended something crucial about the nature and function of biblical narrative that will change the way they hear these stories forever. It's not just Bible stories anymore.

That's "why-to" learn something about exploratory ensemble storytelling.

Each chapter of this book is both a "how-to" and a "why-to" chapter. The "how-to" exercises and examples are selected so as to give glimpses of the "why-to." I do not pretend that these exercises and examples are the only suitable ones, but I do suggest that you engage them carefully and look for both the "how-to" and the "why-to" factors before substituting your own exercises or examples. This book is up to something, and you will get more out of reading it if you remember that vigorously. Everything is doubled.

Each chapter is doubled in another way as well. Each chapter roots itself in an exceedingly practical aspect of exploratory ensemble storytelling. Thus chapter 1 takes up the matter of remembering the story, which is perhaps what keeps most people from taking up the practice of biblical storytelling in the first place. "How could you possibly remember all of that?" storytellers are commonly asked. Chapter 2 considers the matter of the space between bodies. Ensemble storytelling requires that members of the ensemble have somewhere to stand, and that where they stand and how they relate to each other have a meaning for the story. This is basic stuff. Likewise chapter 3 deals with the basic matter of how one selects an interpretive line to follow. I argue that the only way to go wrong is to determine ahead of time never to make a mistake. As Martin Luther said, "Sin boldly, and believe more boldly still." Chapter 4 finishes this short process by examining the issue of narrative arc and coherence. As Benjamin Franklin said in an altogether unrelated context, "Either we must hang together, or we shall surely all hang separately."

Thus all the chapters provide practical answers for the question that gives birth to the first chapter: How do you remember all this? You remember it by giving the words a physical home in your body, by taking these stories of real human bodies and re-membering them in the members of the real human bodies of the ensemble (chapter 1). (This is the process that Tom Boomershine calls "learning by heart" as opposed to "memorizing." I find his distinction exceedingly helpful.) You remember it by placing the words in bodies that relate to each other in space (chapter 2). I have found that if you can get the relational space right between the members of the ensemble, the scene takes place and the words take care of themselves. I also find that memory problems are often really problems with the staging of the scene. If this is indeed true, then in order to remember the words it will be necessary to hunt widely for ways to embody and stage them (chapter 3). Some of the standard ways of reading biblical narratives work badly when you try to play them. Actors can't learn their lines, and the scenes remain unpersuasive. We commit ourselves to making productive mistakes as part of the simple practical work of looking for ways to play the scene, ways that work. And finally, you remember the words much more effectively when you comprehend them as part of a followable narrative arc, as part of a story that does indeed "hang together" (chapter 4).

At the same time, however, each chapter is up to something else. Each chapter is thoroughly practical, but each chapter is also deeply theoretical. Each of these practical investigations, each of the suggestions, exercises, and examples is rooted in literary and performance theory. This theoretical background is wide-ranging and varied. But it all comes together around the practice of telling these stories in exploratory ensembles.

Thus chapter 1, "Re-Membering the Story," draws on ritual studies as well as recent work in the philosophy and theology of body. If the performing of a ritual re-members a character from the past, makes her a member of the present community, then the performing of a biblical story will also accomplish something similar. Think of the way ritual and narrative are wound together in the Passover. Year after year, Jews tell the story and place themselves in it: "A wandering Aramean was my father . . ." If performance of a story re-members a character from the past when that character is embodied in a player, then it will matter in what body that character is placed. When Jesus refuses to heal a woman's daughter because the woman is a gentile, Syrophoenician by birth, it will play differently if the woman's character is embodied by a young white woman than if she is embodied by an older African American woman. Body makes a difference, in real life and in exploratory ensemble telling of biblical stories.

Likewise the space between the bodies will matter, and I explore this space in chapter 2, "Taking Place . . . Taking Up Space." Space between the bodies in a scene is not just an empty nothing. The space between bodies is tense with encounters and refusals, sculpted out of angles, levels, and distances. For instance, if the Syrophoenician woman looks Jesus in the eye when she speaks, the scene plays one way. If she cringes on the ground while speaking it plays another. This chapter is informed by the work of Emmanuel Levinas, who understood ethics to be born in the tense space between human faces. What does it mean for the exploration of biblical stories that Jesus has to look, or not look, at the face of this Other, this gentile, this mother, this woman, when he speaks about feeding children and dogs?

In the third chapter, "How To Make Mistakes," I explore the multiplicity that is embedded in every text. Interpreters and other storytellers wouldn't need to think about making mistakes if texts made simple, straightforward sense. If texts were simple, interpreters would only have to worry about getting things right. The problem is that it is not easy to make sense; in fact, it requires strenuous effort. As literary theorists have suggested, every text, however coherent, frays and unravels sometimes. Sometimes this shows up in the tension that can be found between a character's nature in different scenes. Sometimes David is gentle and sometimes he is calculating. To tell the story of David effectively and with integrity, a player will have to find a way to honor these tensions, perhaps by making mistakes and playing the gentle scenes as if he were cold and calculating instead. Sometimes this tension, however, creeps into a character's lines, even within an individual scene. This word sounds kind and that phrase sounds harsh. The content of this speech is comforting but the metaphors continually flirt with images of destruction. I have found that literary theorists offer great help at this point. They have provided us with tools sharp enough to probe these tensions and to make diagnostic distinctions about the tone and flavor of the language being used. Making mistakes is sometimes the best way to point out these distinctions.

Chapter 4, "Holding Together/Coming Apart," takes this analysis of tension to a larger stage. If making sense is sometimes complicated in small scenes, it is also difficult when one considers whole narratives. Literary theorists have lately abandoned the practice of speaking of (and analyzing) whole narratives because of their acute awareness of the ways texts break into shards and shatter. This is where this way of engaging biblical stories becomes particularly productive. This, indeed, is where the practical and theoretical aspects of this book become most deeply engaged with each other.

Literary analysts have noted (accurately) the ways texts break against themselves. At the same time, performers are charged with delivering a whole performance, a completed narrative arc, a show that hangs together. This is their charge and their practice, even if it were only a matter of learning and performing their lines. I once had a student attempt to perform Samuel Beckett's work "Ping" (a fascinatingly incoherent bit of coherence). The student, in order to learn his lines, did what critical interpreters have also done with this work: they all created little narrative arcs, little local explanations that they used to explain why this word followed that word and fit into a larger pattern that they "discovered." The student decided (as have other interpreters) that "Ping" was a Jesus story and he found every bit of evidence he could to support that reading of the "whole" story. Only then could he learn it. And only then, he said (echoing Aristotle without knowing it), could an audience be expected to make sense of it. "They need a beginning, a middle, and an end," he said, "something to take them from one place to another." Both Aristotle and my student were right. And chapter 4 uses the best resources from theory and practice to focus attention on how and why it is productive to practice telling whole biblical stories.

Do you need to be thoroughly at home in the wilds of literary theory to make sense of this book? Of course not. At most points the theoretical considerations can simply be seen dancing on a distant hillside. They are there to be looked at if you should so choose, but the practical matters will provide plenty of interesting diversion for you. This book is driven by the conviction that embodiment is the best starting point for biblical interpretation, and that means that the best door into all matters theoretical is a thoroughly practical engagement with the stories. You will find, however, that the practical exercises and examples are thoroughly informed by the theoretical explorations that arise from this work. Because this is true, I owe you a good glimpse of how theory and practice might dance together. I also owe you a map of a path you might follow if you wanted to dance on the distant hillside with the theories that give life to this work. That map starts in the practical exercises and examples, continues in the text of the chapters, and issues finally in reading suggestions that would allow you (whatever your background or interest) to find your way further into such considerations.

What should you expect from this book? Expect an attention to matters of "how-to" and "why-to." Expect a practical process that takes bodies and real life seriously. Expect to catch the sound of theoretical music drifting on the breeze at any moment.

Expect to learn why and how to tell biblical stories. Expect also, as you learn, to be provoked. (You will have guessed at this from the title of the book.) There are theological reasons for this. As I read biblical narrative, I notice a preference on God's part for the springing of surprises. Sarah and Abraham's son Isaac wasn't named "Laughter" because of his sunny disposition. Isaac's birth in Sarah's old age was a surprise, and a provocation, and not the last such provocation in the history of this family. Any responsible theology flowing from the stories of this family will also have to expect provocation.

There are also simple practical reasons for this provocation. This kind of storytelling flirts with the theater, and actors and directors know that if there is no provocation, no clash, the audience will never come back from intermission.

That is finally what this book is meant to do. I believe that biblical narrative has too often been made so mild-mannered, so tame, so foreign to its own nature that the audience has gone out to intermission and stayed there. If biblical stories are actually a central way that God (and God's people) resist brutality and tell counter-stories that nurture humanity, then we had better find a way to get the audience back. My class working with creation stories realized this. They discovered in Genesis 2 a story told to heal the creation in the aftermath of terrible violence. This book is offered as a contribution to that worthy, and complicated, effort. It's not just Bible stories anymore.

1

Re-Membering the Story

You don't have anything,
if you don't have the stories.

—Leslie Marmon Silko, *Ceremony*

PART ONE: WHY TO RE-MEMBER THE STORY

Remember.

That is what human communities ask of their members. The aim is to deepen the community's sense of itself beyond the current, transient population. The aim is to link the people who come and go, the crises that come and go, the joys that come and go with a past that provides orientation and understanding, provides a sense of the stars and of how to steer by them. Remember: even the word reveals something of the dance that is involved. Those people that have been part of the community in the past are to be made continuing members of the community's present; they are to be re-membered, as it were. Those events that members of the community have shared and suffered and survived are to be held as an inheritance, a form of life into which current members of the community are drawn.

And so the town in which I grew up placed a Sherman tank on the courthouse lawn, placed it next to the statue of a Civil War soldier who stood, leaning wearily on his rifle, above the names of those from our town who had died in that war, the names we were to re-member. And so also the children in the town played on the tank, which, though all its moving parts were welded and frozen, was still a way of touching something our parents had known, something just beyond our reach. For a child born, as I was, in 1952, World War II was everywhere around us and it was clear that it was our task to re-member it. And so we played on the tank, practicing to be members of the community into which we had been placed. We played at war in order to remember, at least until we were told to stop.

And we were, indeed, told to stop, which was also part of the re-membering. Our games touched memories that were painful and dangerous beyond our understanding. We saw that pain and danger, and learned also to re-member them. And so we learned not to ask to hear stories about the war. There were stories to be told, to be sure, and we would hear some and guess at others, but we learned that there were stories we would not hear, things not suited for children. We learned that we were surrounded by stories that we would not hear, maybe not ever. This also was part of remembering. When we marched in the Memorial Day parade, every member of the Boy Scout troop knew that we were remembering the stories that our scoutmaster would never tell, our scoutmaster who could not march with us because he had lost the use of his legs in a battle we would never hear about. We marched for him, to re-member. We knew that we would not ask about the uncle who had not returned from Guadalcanal or about the man in our town who found his brother washed up on Omaha Beach. We marched to re-member them. And we learned, from whispered, mostly legendary tales, that remembering went on over too many beers at the bar in the American Legion post, a place where children could not go until they were also old enough to have things to remember and forget.

And so, also, we have made movies and have watched them, we have written stories and have read them: *'Til the End of Time, The Longest Day, The Victors, Slaughterhouse Five, The Naked and the Dead, Catch 22,*

Saving Private Ryan, The Greatest Generation—these and many others. Some of the movies, some of the stories came out shortly after the war. Some came out many years later. Some were meant for children, some definitely were not. But all of them, all the stories, all the movies, all the remembering shaped the games we played as children, the imaginings we carried with us into adulthood.

But our task here is to explore the ways Jesus was re-membered. The situations are different, obviously: different centuries, different cultures, different languages, different circumstances. Above all, these phenomena are vastly different in scale. In the one case, the issue is global warfare involving hundreds of millions of people and tens of millions of deaths. In the other case, there is only one person, and only one death. The one involves a global cataclysm. The other is tiny by comparison, though it was to have global consequences and involves its own sort of cataclysm, as will be seen in later chapters. But for now it is enough to note that, for all the decisive differences, the modes of re-membering were largely the same. There were monuments and occasions for marching. There were communities spread across a wide area that were involved in remembering, recovering, and reflecting. And, central to this large and sprawling process, there were stories. There were stories because there were people and patterns in danger of being lost. Jesus had left the scene. Many of his followers, named in the gospels, were (very shortly) dead, as well. The Temple was gone, and with it a whole stable world that needed remembering. In the face of such threats, human beings work to re-member that which has been lost, to add depth to the transient present. And so there were stories.

There were stories also because that is the way communities choose to work through matters requiring the most difficult thought. The Temple was, indeed, gone. That loss, perhaps more than any other, shook the world of Jews and of those affiliated with them, and that shaking required careful and difficult rethinking. Add to that the social, cultural, and theological earthquakes associated with the growth of the Christian movement(s) that had led to a confusing variety of ways to understand the world, again for Jews and those affiliated with them, whether part of the Christian movement(s) or not. And at the core of all this upheaval was a messiah who had been crucified and whose career had not led to the sort of balance and stability that God's people would expect from God's visitation of the world. The poor were still with them, and the Romans were still in power. This, too, called for the telling of stories, because we tell stories for at least two different reasons: to re-member that which we cannot lose, and to resolve that which we cannot stop thinking about.

And So We Tell Stories

Frank Kermode has made helpful sense of these paired functions of stories. The one he calls "myth." Myths give depth to the present moment because they explain why things are the way they are. They anchor the fleeting moment in a patterned dance that stretches back into ancient memory. The other sort of story he calls "fiction." These are the stories human communities tell in order to figure things out.[1] At first glance, this word seems ill-suited for this use because in typical English usage it carries the notion of falsehood. Behind the English word, however, there vibrates a notion carried by the Latin, *fictrix/fictor*: one who forms or fashions. Through the work of a *fictrix* something formless is shaped into something useful, suitable, serviceable, and real.[2] A potter takes something malleable, something on which a human being can work, and makes it into something *with which* a human being can work. There is in this activity no falsification. Clay is not truer or more virtuous than a pot. If anything, the opposite is true.

For Kermode, works of fiction are created (and read) as part of a process of working and reworking something raw, something hard to think about, dangerous, even, until it becomes something that can be comprehended and used, or at least appreciated. Experiences, disasters, and dislocations of sense are worked, shaped, and combined with other things until sense is made, or until sense is seen to have been forever violated. Without this shaping, nothing could be true.

Of course, as anyone who watches political spin-doctors knows, the line between "shaping" and "falsifying" is not always easy to draw with certainty. What looks like helpful elaboration from one partisan side looks like lying from the other. Even when you subtract those cases that clearly involve cynical manipulation of the truth you still have a situation that bears watching. If Kermode is correct and truth comes out of a process of working and reworking raw events, then there will always be a risk that "truth" will be transformed into "whatever they can make you believe."[3]

This risk is real and must be remembered. Aristotle, however, provides a more helpful context in which to think about this activity. As is clear from the *Poetics*, raw experience is unthinkable, and therefore unprofitable. Out of the vast randomness of actual events, a poet constructs a plot that does not begin at a random point and does not conclude at a random point; rather, it is built (shaped) into a finished work that has a beginning, a middle, and an end. "The function of a poet," says Aristotle, "[is] to relate not things that have happened, but things that may happen." It is for this reason, Aristotle says, that "poetry is a more philosophical and more serious thing than history."[4] Until raw experience is shaped, molded,—"fict-ed"—it cannot be true or false because it cannot be thought.

The question is, of course, are the gospels to be understood, in Kermode's terms, as myth or as fiction? The answer is, probably, that they were both, sometimes simultaneously. One need only note the attempt to use a mythic structure ("it is necessary")[5] to stabilize the most recalcitrant aspect of Jesus' career (his rejection and death by crucifixion). In the face of certain objections from anyone who knew what crucifixion entailed, and from everyone who knew what being called "Messiah" ought to entail,[6] Mark asserts that there is no problem. In fact, things are the way they are (Jesus is crucified) because it is simply necessary. This assertion of mythic stability, however, is not myth at all but a careful application of fiction, an experimental shaping of raw material, a shaping driven by a need to figure out something that did not make sense. The crucifixion was a dangerous obscenity that required continual attention from Christian speakers and writers throughout the early period of the Christian movement(s), as can be seen from Christian texts and from taunts directed at the Christian movement(s).[7] One ought also to note that what may have begun as an exercise in Kermodian fiction becomes the most stable sort of myth when the struggle driving it is forgotten. Once every Sunday school child knows that it is obviously necessary that the messiah should die, and that the death makes perfect sense in the context of some eternal economy in which the messiah's death pays for human sin, once the death is no longer troublesome (or moronic, as Paul calls it in 1 Corinthians[8]), then the gospels become myths that explain quite simply why things must always be the way they are. This would, in passing, imply that such forgetting, and such readings of the gospels, vigorously misunderstand the narratives, because they mistake the genre from the very start. Myths and fictions operate very differently and call for different reading and interpretive strategies.

Choosing Story

We tell stories to preserve the past and also to make sense of it. And so it was that when Christians in the ancient world set out to remember Jesus, they chose story. Four times, four different times (considering only the canonical gospels for the moment) they chose stories. And they chose stories that are significantly different from each other (differently fict-ed, one might say). To be sure, the gospels share many similarities: the Synoptics share a rough outline (variously explained) and all the canonical gospels share the basic understanding that this is a story about Jesus who was crucified and raised from death. But beyond that, even in the Synoptics, the differences are sometimes surprising. There are major differences in what the Russian Formalists called the *fabula* of the story,[9] the basic set of events that can be laid out chronologically by a diligent reader. The easiest place to see this is at the beginning and end of each story. The Christmas story in Mark or John would take very little time to read during worship, given that it is not there. The events that are part of the postresurrection sections of each of the gospels are wildly assorted. John ends twice so as to include more. Mark ends five different ways because he includes so little. Matthew and Luke have endings that complete their individual stories, but that would immediately leap forward as out of place were they to be interchanged.

The differences extend to smaller matters. What did it mean that Jesus grew up in Nazareth? In Matthew, he lived there because his family was forced to flee there. Matthew tells a story of Jesus the refugee, whose original home was Bethlehem. In Luke, quite to the contrary, Jesus lives in Nazareth because that is where his parents lived. They only traveled to Bethlehem for the census. Bethlehem was, indeed, Joseph's ancestral home, but Nazareth was his own home, and that of Jesus and Mary. The difference is important for the story. Another instance: how many times did Jesus visit Jerusalem? In Mark, as Ernst Lohmeyer noted, Jesus comes to Jerusalem, which Lohmeyer calls the "source of all enmity against Jesus,"[10] only at the end of his career. In Luke, we see

Jesus in Jerusalem at least two more times, just after birth and at the age of bar mitzvah, and we are given the implication that he and his family went there, as was their custom, annually. This difference also matters, especially when Jesus is approaching Jerusalem at the end of the story. Is he headed toward a forbidding place, a foreign place filled with threat? Or is he heading toward a place that he could tell stories about from childhood memories? The differences matter, even when the gospels follow similar outlines.

But the differences did not lead to the homogenization of the stories. The four canonical gospels sit next to each other, each different, each distinct, each claimed as true. In fact, attempts to erase the differences were specifically rejected by the Christian movement. When Tatian, in the second century, wove the four gospels into one unified story, the effect was declared to be heretical. The differences, the dissonances, were judged to be essential, despite the difficulties they created. In fact, Irenaeus, writing also in the second century, said that there were four gospels for the same reason that there were four winds. The wholeness of the world, and the realities of human activity and commerce required it.[11]

When Christians in the ancient world set out to remember Jesus authoritatively and effectively, they chose story. They did not do this, as one sometimes senses in older commentaries, because the ancient world, unlike the modern, was simpler and so was dependent on the narrative form.[12] The ancient world had many ways to remember things that mattered. Lists, for example, are a perfectly good way to remember things in the ancient world, as in the contemporary world. We have a great many lists preserved from the ancient world, lists that preserved one sort of memory or another: business records, membership rolls, significant events. We even have a gospel in the form of a list, the gospel of Thomas, discovered in 1945 near the town of Nag Hammadi. The gospel of Thomas is not a narrative. There is no plot, no beginning, no ending. There is only a list of 114 short episodes. Most episodes contain no more than a saying of Jesus. Some begin with a short narrative lead-in:

His disciples said to him, "When will the rest for the dead take place, and when will the new world come?" (Thom. 51)[13]

Following that, there is a nugget, a pithy saying, something decisive. Then the episode concludes and the next saying begins straightaway.

The gospel of Thomas is an important document in the study of the gospels. It has contributed mightily to our understanding of Jesus' parables, and it continues to be significant for those scholars who are engaged in Q studies. It offers a view of Jesus perhaps rooted in the Jewish Wisdom tradition, a picture of "incipient Gnosticism."[14] It is of great value as an artifact from the ancient world, as a glimpse of the richness of the stream of tradition that flowed around the character, Jesus. But it is significant to note that the gospel did not attain wider use than it did.

There will have been many reasons that Thomas was not more widely accepted, reasons ranging from geography to sociology to theology. Much that is to be found in the gospel will be familiar to contemporary readers, such as the parables that appear throughout the text. Some of them are in forms very like the form familiar to readers of the canonical gospels. Some of them are similar, but strikingly different. For instance, the parable of the lost sheep appears in Thomas:

> Jesus said, The imperial rule is like a shepherd who had a hundred sheep. One of them, the largest, went astray. He left the ninety-nine and looked for the one until he found it. After he had toiled, he said to the sheep, "I love you more than the ninety-nine." (Thom. 107)

The difference, the oddity, is everywhere to be felt. One sheep was lost. It was the largest.[15] One might well speculate that this is the way a community would tell the story if it were convinced that it was the most valuable sheep, though isolated and rejected by the rest of the flock. The parable is recognizable, but odd.

The best oddity of all comes in the last saying in the list. Mary has been told by Simon Peter that she, being a woman, has no place in the kingdom. Jesus enters the scene, as he always does in Thomas, and solves the problem that has been encountered.

> Simon Peter said to them, "Make Mary leave us, for females don't deserve life."
> Jesus said, "Look, I will guide her to make her male, so that she too may become a living spirit resembling you males. For every

female who makes herself male will enter the domain of Heaven. (Thom. 114)

This is adequately odd. But I would like to suggest that it was not oddity that limited the acceptance of Thomas in the wider church. Examination of the Bible makes it clear enough that oddity doesn't seem to be a reason for excluding anything. I would like to suggest, playfully at least, that Thomas did not become part of the canon, not because it is odd, but because it is not a story.[16] This suggestion surely overplays the evidence, but it is intriguing to follow Irenaeus's argument in Against Heresies. He makes repeated reference to points of philosophy, theology, and ideology as he rejects those groups that hold to other gospels, or to other forms of the gospels Irenaeus holds to be true and approved, and these points are clearly the reasons that he rejects the positions he identifies. At the same time, when he argues against Marcion he accuses him of mutilating Luke's gospel, which he surely did. And his argument against "those following Valentinus" likewise supposes that the whole narrative provides criteria for judging the validity of those who make "copious use" of the gospel according to John. It is no hindrance that the borders between community, ideology, and text are blurred here, since this blurring must always take place as part of any reading. We always read from where we are, and with reference to who we are.[17] Community and text always merge and mix, back and forth. What matters for this playful argument is that Irenaeus uses the wholeness of the narrative as a standard to judge competing communities and their gospels. Perhaps a similar judgment was made regarding Thomas. It is not a whole narrative. Judging from the biblical evidence, both Jews and Christians have a huge commitment to story. The gospels, of course, are narrative. The Pentateuch is narrative; the Deuteronomic books are narrative. The Writings contain narrative. The Prophets have embedded narratives, and larger, enveloping implied narratives, as do the letters of Paul. Even Revelation takes the form of a narrative, though an odd one. Thomas is not. And it is not included.

If narrative form is so significant that it might even be taken seriously as a criterion for inclusion or exclusion from the canon, then it will be important to examine carefully what stories do that lists (and other forms of literature) do not.

CHAPTER ONE

The Power of Reading

Stories do many things. I want to suggest three of the most important.

First of all, stories project worlds. When you pick up a story and read it, the words do not stay put on the page. They are blown off the page by the force of the story, they sweep out from the book and they envelop the reader. They create a whole, convincing world. This power affects readers differently. All feel it, though some feel it more faintly.

And some of us are overwhelmed by it. I have been deeply susceptible to story all my life. When I was a child, I would rather read than do dishes, rather read than eat, rather read than play baseball. This worried my parents. I remember one day when I was about twelve years old. I was lying on the couch reading a book, probably a mystery. My mother came into the room and, being a good and attentive mother, told me to go outside and play. "I can't," I said. "It's raining." It was January. It was Minnesota, and the temperature outside was probably below zero. It was only raining in the book that I was reading. When stories project worlds, those worlds are completely convincing for me. Not all readers are so susceptible, but even for the most casual reader the words refuse simply to stay put on the page.

Second, stories do not only project worlds, they draw readers into those worlds. That is, of course, what makes those worlds so convincing, especially to those of us who are susceptible. Everyone has books on their shelves with bookmarks about thirty-five pages in, maybe sixty pages in. The bookmarks have yellowed with age. The bindings of the books are arthritic, and the bookmarks have not moved in years. Why? The reader was not drawn into the book. But probably all of us have had another experience as well. Probably all of us have sometime picked up a book, intending to read just long enough to get sleepy. An hour later, we read for just another chapter. An hour later, we intended just to finish the page we were on. Three hours later the sun was coming up. Why? The book drew us in, and we could not get back out.

Some of the best illustrations of this power have been created by Michael Ende. In his book, *The Neverending Story*, Ende introduces to his readers a young boy, Bastian Balthazar Bux, a young boy with an impossible life. In order to escape both bullies and difficulties related to the death of his mother, Bastian ducks into a bookstore. He steals a book, a beautiful book, sneaks into the attic of his school, locks the door, and begins to read. At midnight, he suddenly finds himself inside the story he is reading. The world projected by the story becomes his world, and he spends the rest of the story trying to find his way back out. He comes close to failing. Stories are that powerful.

What is it that pulls you into a story that you are reading? Perhaps it is suspense. As you read, you can feel something hanging over your head. The story spins its way through complication after complication, the plot (and it really is a kind of conspiracy) of the story catches you, surprises you, and makes you wait. And the sense that something is about to fall on you gets stronger and stronger. Pages fly by, and time, too. You watch details, you look for hints, warnings that something is ready to fall. And you keep on reading.

Perhaps it is character. Some writers have created characters so delightful that you keep on reading just to remain in their company. For me, the characters in Dorothy Sayers's Lord Peter Wimsey mysteries are like that. Harriet Vane's strength, Lord Peter's casual humor, the fact that the characters develop, actually change, from book to book and in the course of the story, all this draws me into the stories. The characters, further, are so rounded, so human, that I find myself believing that you could ask them any question at all, even questions irrelevant to the story, and they would be able to answer. Perhaps other kinds of character effects draw your continued attention.

Maybe it is simply the language of the story. I just like the way some novels taste. The words seem sweet, or pungent, or spicy. They dance together in a subtle play of flavors that has led me to read even stories about which I care little, just to keep tasting the language. Or maybe it is something about the setting of the story. Or maybe it's the detail, historical or biographical or geographical. Whatever it is, pay attention to it. The things that draw you into other stories will also draw you into gospel stories. It is helpful to know what is happening to you.

To extend this a bit, once stories draw you into their world, they provide for you a place to stand, a platform from which you can watch the parade of the story. From the angle of view provided, you can tell which characters you should like, and which you should distrust. You can tell what projects in the story are likely to turn out well, and which are likely to end in crumbling failure. You can tell what viewpoints you are expected to agree with, and which you are expected to oppose.[18] It should

11

be noted that you are not, by any means, required to stand on the platform for the whole while you are reading. You are, in fact, quite free to move about and read from other angles. You are even free to read against the grain of the story. But wherever you stand, reliable interpretation requires that you know where you are with reference to the platform the story intended for you to stand on.

The third power that stories have is the most important of all. Stories do not only project worlds. They do not only draw you into those worlds, providing a place to stand. Most important of all, they create roles, expectations, and ways of seeing the world. This is true within the boundaries of the story. This location is important, but far more important is the way stories carry out this function outside the boundaries of the story.

Stories create roles. That is surely true for the characters within a story, both in a simple descriptive sense and in an analytical, structuralist sense. There are identifiable helpers and opponents, senders and receivers. Even more important than either of these senses, however, is the power that stories have to create roles that readers/hearers carry with them outside the story into the rest of the world they think they live in. When I was a child, we only got two television channels in our town, and both of them were full of cowboys. As a result, my friends and I spent much of our TV time living in a cowboy world.

We watched Roy Rogers. We watched the Lone Ranger. We watched Hop-along Cassidy. We watched Red Ryder. And, of course, when the shows were over, we gathered in the vacant lot down the street and played (you guessed it) cowboys.

Every generation has its own equivalent set of stories. Maybe it was the Ninja Turtles for you. Maybe it was the Power Rangers. Maybe Pokemon. Maybe some story or character I have never heard of. Each set of stories comes with its own liabilities, its own problems.

And each set comes with its own rules. Cowboy stories take place in a cowboy world. This world imposes its own set of activities, rules, and roles. To live in a cowboy world, you are required to be able to ride and rope and shoot. When my friends and I met in the vacant lot, we were ridin', ropin', and shootin' fools. None of us owned a horse. No one even owned a rope. We had never shot anything. We were after all only eight years old. But when we met to play cowboys, we were all perfectly capable of shooting the eye out of a squirrel at three hundred yards. What granted us that amazing capability? The story created us as beings fully capable of these feats, and even greater ones.

Most important of all, the stories made us able to do the most important thing of all in cowboy stories: act nobly. Week after week we risked incredible danger, stood up to unbelievable odds, even laid down our lives for our friends, all because these activities were required by the cowboy world we were playing. We were ordinary kids from southern Minnesota; we didn't know noble from nothing. The stories, however, created that knowledge, that ability, in us and for us.

Stories also create expectations. In the cowboy world, people just want to live "peaceable-like," when all of a sudden terrible violence erupts in the middle of the world. Simple, good people are suddenly in danger. Such situations require only one thing (in cowboy thinking): someone has to stand up and "do what's right." Week after week, we took turns standing up and doing what's right. The stories created the role we played. They also created the expectation that the world was a place where violence could erupt at any time. If this expectation were limited to vacant lots and childhood, stories would still be powerful. These expectations, however, extend far beyond childhood. This power of stories becomes important when it extends into a reader's way of understanding the world, even unconsciously, into adulthood. (Ever feel an overwhelming urge to stand up and "do what's right"?) Sometimes the effect comes from stories that are experienced from adult reading. Sometimes the effect is a holdover from childhood reading. In any case, human beings carry with them roles, expectations, and ways of seeing the world that they try out, consciously or otherwise, throughout their lives.

Finally, stories create durable ways of seeing the world. Everyone sees the world in more than one way. We all live with floating levels of dissonance among the worldviews we find native. But though these views are multiple, they are limited, not by the world, but by our limited apprenticeship to the world. If we think primarily in German, it has effects on the way we organize our linguistic worlds, giving us (perhaps) an infinite patience as we wait for verbs. If we think primarily in Lakota, we think without English verb tenses, and with a consequently different view of time than we would have if we thought primarily in

English. If we thought primarily in Gaelic, where one does not say, "He opens the door," but rather, "He is present at the opening of the door," we might well think of the world as the plain on which rigidly deterministic forces maneuver.

Stories afford the possibility of expanding beyond our naturally limited repertoires of views and apprenticeships. A story that was conceived in a language other than our primary language will, even in (good) translation, open us to a different way of seeing the world, a different way of holding sequence and suspension together. A story written (or better: spoken) from within a gender or a sexual orientation other than our own will create in our eyes a vision we would never otherwise have. In story we can experiment and explore where we would never otherwise go.

This, of course, raises the question of what durable effect stories might have on the way we view the world. Wolfgang Iser, in a most helpful study, examines the ways the stories we prefer reveal who we are. He calls this area of study "literary anthropology."[19] We choose our stories on purpose. Our choices reinforce our being. From another angle, Wayne Booth, in *The Company We Keep*, examines more specific effects of specific narratives. His appendix focusing on feminist readings of Rabelais is especially useful. The fiction of Rabelais makes several lists for essential reading in Western culture. By some definitions, it is "classic" fiction. It is also, as Booth points out, fiction that offered a significant protest against a sexually repressive society and contributed to a more honest and open view of the roles of women and men in society. Still, as Booth notes, we do not read Rabelais in any age other than this one, and we do not encounter his ways of viewing the world in any world but our own. This means that his portrayal of women, and his use of them in his projected worlds means what it means now, and historicist attempts to appreciate the jokes he tells at the expense of women cannot blunt the effect those jokes have on us as we read them: now. When a male character grinds up the genitals of a dog in heat and sprinkles the essence of this concoction on a woman in the story, which has the effect one might predict, contemporary readers must ask about the effect of such a story on the way women and men see each other now.[20]

Likewise, the plots (conspiracies) that shape the stories we tell shape the ways we see complications, threats, and solutions in the world we think we live in. Richard Slotkin, in his book *Gunfighter Nation,* has examined in some detail the way American culture and stories of the American West are fitted to each other. Jane Tompkins has examined similar phenomena. In Westerns, whether in a book or on the screen, the hero is provoked, insulted, attacked. He never retaliates. Then finally the villains push things too far, and "retaliatory violence becomes not simply justifiable but imperative: now, we are made to feel, not to transgress the interdict against violence would be the transgression." "Why," asks Tompkins, "does the Western tell this story over and over?"[21] This is precisely the right question. The answer, she argues, is to be found in the way we carry this plot structure out into regular life, where it gives us what Tompkins calls the "moment of righteous ecstasy, the moment when you know you have the moral advantage of your adversary, the moment of murderousness."[22]

The reader or teller of biblical narrative would do well to similarly examine the stories we tell ourselves. What is the effect of telling this story over and over? This also is just the right question, because all the powers of any story, and all the complications that go with reading, pertain also to biblical narratives.

They pertain, for instance, to the gospel of Mark. Mark's story is as powerful and as complicated as any Western, but reading Mark is all made more complicated by the antiquity of the story, by its long, variegated history of reading, and by the fact that is read not simply as a classic but as Scripture, which yields its own rich set of complications, contradictions, and disagreements. Interpreters must therefore ask the same basic questions they ask of any narrative. How *do* the plots work? What is the basic conspiracy of the story? How are tensions created and resolved? What role does violence play in resolving or creating tensions? What are readers conditioned to hope for, to wait for, by the way the story dances itself out? And, how does this story dance with all the other stories we cannot stop thinking about?

The Power of Telling

So far the effects of remembering Jesus in story pertain to inscribed stories, and then to other forms by extension. Another crucial implication is revealed particularly when the story is not simply read, but told. I find the arguments of Thomas Boomershine, Joanna Dewey, and many others thoroughly persuasive. The gospels were composed as a story to be told. When Mark says in an aside, "Let the reader understand," the reader he is speaking to is the teller of the story who would have performed the text as was typical in the ancient world. The text as we have it represents not a patchwork of oral fragments but an oral composition, either a base text for oral performance or a distillation of an oral performance. The proper form of the gospel is as an oral/aural text, a text that is spoken, heard, performed.

This matters for interpretation because when a story is told, remembering becomes something more than simple recording and reading. When the story is told, remembering becomes re-membering. That is to say, Jesus is made to be physically present, at least provisionally, during the telling of the story. I recall thinking, as a child, that the man up front in church wearing the odd white robe was Jesus. I recall not believing it when I was told otherwise. The things he said and did as part of worship convinced me that he was Jesus in the flesh. Children often make such mistakes. When a story is told, however, something more significant happens, something more durable. When Jesus is embodied in the story that is told, and particularly when the story is played by an ensemble (which allows separation between characters and voices), then Jesus is brought back into the community that re-members him in a vivid and vigorous way. For the duration of the story, Jesus is not an idea but a physical presence with a voice and a body, a location and a presence. The kind of remembrance that can be heard in Christian practices surrounding Holy Communion is extended also to a sort of sacramental presence found in story. If the bread and wine are, in some sense, Jesus' body and blood, then so, too, is the telling of the story a kind of narrative incarnation.

But there is another consequence of this kind of making Jesus physically present. If Jesus is physically brought (in performance) into the contemporary community that re-members him, he must then also be brought into contact with cultural and interpretive matters that he would never have had to deal with in his own native world. If Jesus is physically present in the community through telling his story, he is (in a sense) available for questions after the telling is done and before the next telling begins. Actors (maybe especially in soap operas) often report that their fans speak to them as if they were, in fact, the character they play. Once a literary character is embodied, re-membered as it were, she is really here and really present in the real world. Here Booth's discussion of the demands of reading Rabelais in our contemporary world applies also to Mark's story about Jesus. Some of the questions might surprise the Jesus who walked, and ate, and slept, and scratched where it itched, but when he is re-membered he becomes a member of the present community, which (though shifting and transient) is certainly real, and is the community of which Jesus is now a member. And, as such, he is made to answer questions about which he would have known nothing, and maybe even cared little. The same thing happens in standard interpretation. The issues that interpreters bring to gospel stories shift through time, as they should. But the effect is more vivid still when a storyteller (or better, an ensemble) attempts not just to read, but to *tell* those same stories, to give flesh again to Jesus who now has to react to a new world.

Some of this happens simply because of the demands of telling a story. The teller has to remember the story, a demand that is customarily taken (by audience members) to be a feat of memory, and memory is imagined (popularly) to be a purely mental function: disembodied, intellectual, made up of a flow of words that are mastered by sheer repetition. Repetition is surely part of learning to remember a story, but here Thomas Boomershine has made a most helpful distinction. He notes that a storyteller does not "memorize" a story, but rather learns it by heart. Memorization, says Boomershine, is imagined to be a purely mental function. "Learning by heart" involves taking the story into the teller's body, re-membering it, as it were.[23] The story then can be told because it is embodied. Gestures, movements, postures, physical attitudes are all part of knowing a story by heart, since learning a story involves anchoring it to these bodily realities. But this anchoring brings the story into contact with all the other gestures, movements, postures, and physical attitudes, all the states of physical being that are the stuff of regular life.

If Jesus is re-membered in the process, then it is the storyteller who must do the re-membering. It is the storyteller who must physically discover how it is that the characters in the story, particularly Jesus, can physically say and do what is narrated in the story. This seems obvious at first glance, but practice has proved that it is anything but obvious.

The text is loaded with physical reality: people move from place to place (and quickly, especially in the gospel of Mark), healings and other significant actions *take place* (note the physical, spatial metaphor). There is even considerable report of Jesus' physical reactions in the midst of the events taking place. To be sure, we are given no voyeuristic tour of his inner life, but what we are given is more important. The language is loaded with organ-specific reference to Jesus' reactions and attitudes. He scolds and rebukes, he also snorts like a horse in indignation, and when confronted with a leper his bowels react.[24] Each of these reactions has a powerful physical basis, a location, and a noticeable physical effect. It is noteworthy that these reactions appear to translate badly into English.

Sometimes, as in the case of Jesus' bowels, the common English mode of expression is rather tamer. In English, we feel pity, or we are moved to pity,[25] or we might have a sense of sympathy or even empathy, but none of these expressions even hints at the intestinal reactions basic to the Greek word and the Hebrew organismic metaphor behind it.

Sometimes English has a perfectly good way of expressing the gospels' physically vigorous language, but something, perhaps a tradition of pious *a-patheia*, a holy dispassion (or apathy), holds translators, interpreters, and readers back from a straightforward translation of such language. "Snort" becomes "warn;"[26] "rebuked" becomes "gave strict orders."[27] The image is still vigorous enough that readers of the English text will believe interpreters and preachers when they describe the language of the gospels as "rough and vivid," but they cannot catch just how rough or just how vivid.

And sometimes, even when the language is right there on the page, asking to be embodied, readers and storytellers tone it down. They might be motivated also by pious *a-patheia*, which affects theologians with academic credentials and those without. They might also be affected by the calm conventions of public news reading. Americans who watch news reports on television with any regularity have learned two things: the generally approved American accent appears to originate somewhere near Omaha, and the most appalling disaster can be narrated in measured, well-modulated tones. We expect public reading to be dispassionate. Even when reactions are incorporated into the reading, the range is carefully constricted. One does not bring in the wild emotions or harsh tones that are a regular part of outside life. All emotions, when presented at all, are narrated at a discount. "Indignant" is marked down to "angry." "Angry" becomes "annoyed." "Annoyed" becomes "irritated." All the words are there, but the reading passes without endangering the dispassionate detachment that we expect each other, and ourselves, to maintain.

Re-membering the story requires the storyteller to set detachment aside, requires her to embody the physical reactions that the language on the page hands her, requires that those reactions that have been translated into disembodied oblivion be brought back to ornery life. Re-membering requires that the storyteller learn to snort, to command, to rebuke, to feel in her bowels, to learn to do whatever the story hands her. Sometimes this will require simple rummaging around in whatever store of physical reactions the storyteller has available, looking for what it means for her to snort or bellow. Sometimes it will require rummaging around in someone else's store of reactions, because there are characters in the story who are foreign to most of our experience most of the time. Just what does a demon sound like, anyhow? Some among us may know. The rest of us will have to ask. And it's not only demons and violent opponents that cause the trouble for those who would tell gospel stories. Jesus, himself, is troublesome. His range of reactions is sometimes shocking, especially to dispassionate, phlegmatic people who live safe and orderly lives. We may have few occasions to snort or bellow, little need to rebuke, since chiding will usually do the trick, and (if it doesn't) whining would serve just fine. Jesus rebukes; he scolds; he snorts; his commands have a sharpness that sometimes seems on the edge of violence. A storyteller, however safe, sane, orderly, and dispassionate, must find a way to embody words and worlds that are quite foreign, at least if the story is to be respected and told with integrity.

But this brings surprises. Some surprises come in the form of the ordinary oddities and offenses the gospels contain. Especially in the gospel of Mark, Jesus spreads his reactions along a spectrum that is wider than many religious people generally expect. And sometimes the problem is not just the wildness of his reactions, but the suddenness with which they erupt. Jesus can explode (in Mark, in any case) from compassion into something close to rage, and this in the space of only a few verses, sometimes just a few words. The storyteller who would embody these reactions, re-member them, faces a serious challenge. No matter how many commentators explain Jesus' scolding of Peter after Peter identifies him as Christ, still the storyteller has to find a physical way to make sense of what seems a senseless eruption.

There are other surprises here. A storyteller discovers the utter physical seriousness of the story in the course of learning to re-member the story. The gospels are stories of real bodies with real diseases, real disabilities, and it is a story of real healing. They are stories of real touch, and of real power that flows out in reaction to that touch. How does one embody these matters? No amount of discounting will ease this. Touch might bring a sort of healing in our world, but neither therapeutic massage nor the first touch of love (powerful as they are) will have the effect that touch has in the gospels' narrative world. The intractable and the inexorable are putty in Jesus' hands, and a teller who will re-member this story will need to look for ways to make this true. And sometimes there is no touch at all, and still a physical state that yields to nothing is changed at a mere word. This matter surely needs more detailed discussion, especially on the issue of the physical and social assumption that disability needs healing in the first place and the consequent complications created for those that style themselves as healers. But note for now that the teller of this story will need to physically discover something of what blindness might mean, or leprosy, or disability, if she is to tell the story with integrity.

And each of the gospels is a story of real death. Though they tell this part of the story quite differently, at the end of each story, Jesus dies. His death is narrated more or less sparsely (depending on the individual gospel), but early hearers of the story may be presumed to have been familiar enough with the mode of his death not to need too much in the way of elaboration. Identifying his death as death by crucifixion will have stirred vivid memories of sights and smells and sounds for many tellers and hearers of this old story. Even something so overlaid with dogmatic clarity has the power to surprise when one must tell the story. Mark's story, in particular, sets up the teller and hearers, lures them into the surprise that death always brings with it: the powerful and wonderfully competent young man of the early story loses all of that power and competence at his death. No amount of dogmatic explanatory overlay can blunt the sharp power of Mark's telling of the death of Jesus. No believing certainty about atonement or substitution or ransom can effectively insulate the teller of Mark's story against the desperate death of Jesus. In Matthew, the shock is different, but similarly severe. In Luke, the shock is made (in some ways) even more severe by Luke's almost desperately calm narrative voice. And John complicates the whole matter with his oddly grand way of telling this violent story. In each case, however, Jesus' death is taken with deep seriousness. In order to tell this story, the teller must recognize the physical and cultural reality that death is, in the story, and in the teller herself. In order to tell this story with integrity, the teller must honor what her body, and the bodies of her hearers, know about death.

Judith Rock, a dance theologian of considerable ability, said at a conference a few years ago that people should not presume to interpret biblical texts until they have been to the circus, and she didn't mean some two-bit circus with three mangy lions and a single geriatric elephant. She meant a real, full-fledged circus with clowns, and horses, and highwire acts. Especially highwire acts. They are important because of what they reveal about the human race. When the tightrope walker steps out onto the wire, she is doing something no one (or almost no one) in the audience would ever do, something no one even could do, no matter the need or the determination. But for all that, tightrope walkers do appear to know their trade. They walk slowly, smoothly, with a cool and distant competence. Too much of this and the act begins to look like an easy stroll back and forth, punctuated by pauses for applause. But then the walker slips. Everyone gasps. Suddenly they all find themselves up on the wire along with her, they all feel in their gut the danger and the fear. Rock says that the human race is joined at the gut, and that this moment, the moment the highwire walker seems about to fall, reveals that basic truth. In order to tell a story of death, no matter how central to the dogmatic and confessional tradition of the faith, a storyteller must recognize and honor what her body knows about real death and real danger.

Perhaps the most important surprise of all comes when the storyteller engages the gospels as stories, not only of real death, but (more important) as stories of real resurrection. There is gathered around the resurrection in each of the gospels a real oddity, a real offense, and a real seriousness that resists all the explanatory interpretations (sometimes they sound almost exculpatory) that we have generated. "They experienced him as raised," "He rose in their hearts"—one often hears such things in sermons. They are quite beside the point for one who would tell the resurrection stories. How does one tell the story of Jesus' resurrection as a true story? This is not a dogmatic question, neither is it a confessional or doctrinal question, at least not for the moment. I mean simply to ask about how one *actually* tells this story as a *true* story. For a storyteller, this is a physical question. The body knows its mortality intimately. This is true even when the teller is young and still charmingly immortal and invulnerable. It becomes even truer when the teller must negotiate reading through bifocals while holding the book with arthritic hands, all the while standing on creaky knees.

The body knows its own mortality as well as the larger human community knows that the possibility of forgetting, of losing members and their past requires a careful practice of remembering. Human being (considered as an activity) knows the reality of loss all too well, and this is true whether you are talking about individual humans or about human communities. We all know this reality, and we demand that it be honored. There is a deep offense to be felt in any telling of any story of resurrection that does not honor the physical reality of death and loss. The names on the Civil War monument in my hometown were real names, real people who died real deaths. The stories that we marched to remember (even when we were never told the story), those also were real stories of real death. The games we played, the stories we told and watched and wrote, the fictions we struggled with: all were rooted in a powerful, gut-level recognition of the implacable, unrepentant reality of the real world, and of real death. We are not patient with any adult who seems not to have learned this yet. Every teller knows this, as does every hearer, so any telling that dodges the stories we must re-member and cannot stop thinking about, will be false from the start. This is, it would seem, the final and most important challenge to the teller of stories about Jesus, to tell the story of resurrection, to re-member it as a true story, as real.

So how does one tell this story as true? The answer is complicated. For now, we should note that wonder is mandatory, but not enough. To tell this story with a kind of breathless wonder threatens to make this into a trick, a dodge, an attempt to tell the audience what to feel. That never works. Wonder at such an impossible event is mandatory, but so may be disbelief, even cynicism, at least if the storyteller aims to honor the real reactions of her audience to such a thing.

Wonder, disbelief, cynicism: and these are just the beginning of the list. Stories of resurrection might also be dangerous stories, since so much of our legal system is built on our fear of death. If a person who was dead is suddenly, somehow alive again, has the border between life and death now become permeable? Will there be others who will return? Who might they be? What might they do to get even with the people who condemned them to death?

Or would a story in which death is reversible make people (the teller included) think differently about life? But how would this change in perspective affect the way the story could be told? Asking such questions will cause trouble, to be sure. But it may be exactly the right sort of trouble. It may be exactly what is required if the task at hand is to provoke the gospel. It may take something that pointed, that real. What other options might there be? There are many, and it will take time, trust, and determined experimentation to find them.

How does one tell stories of resurrection as true stories? For now, let the question ring. It is a mark of adulthood to know that questions worth asking seldom have simple answers. An adult who has lived a real (and, consequently, complicated) life knows that some crucial questions may not have answers at all. But adults who have actually learned something from the complications of their lives have learned that they must still press those questions. For now, a warning: if you are a beginning storyteller, do not rush into telling resurrection stories. Those stories are at the heart of the Christian faith, but if the task is to tell true stories, public stories, stories that take real life (and real death) seriously, then a storyteller learns early on that resurrection stories are going to require both long experience and courageous experimentation. Take the time. Do the experiments. Tell the stories. But make sure that you remember the unrepentant reality of real life and real death.

To remember. This is the task of all human community. To remember so as not to lose and so as to be able to figure out our life together. To remember so as to learn ways to steer by the stars, or so as to find new stars to steer by. To re-member Jesus so as to, one more time, argue for incarnation against bland docetism, even if incarnation means that Jesus must now make a new narrative way through the world, make his way in the face of all those things, those experiences, those joys and disasters that we, as people of memory and integrity, must (these days) also re-member. History and real life did not stop with Jesus' career, no matter what theological arguments are advanced to the contrary. This re-membering will result in both challenges and comforts, both for storytellers and hearers, but (as with all things bodily and remembered) it will not be immediately clear which is challenge and which is comfort.

PART TWO: HOW TO RE-MEMBER THE STORY
Gather an Ensemble

The first thing to do is to gather a group to work with, think with, explore with, and re-member with. You can indeed do all sorts of storytelling as a solo act. Most people do. But the value of this particular way of working with stories emerges most clearly when you work with an ensemble.

So gather a group of people. Make the group interesting. That could mean all sorts of things. I mean everything you've thought of, and more. Gather people who will be fun to think with. Gather more than one gender, people of all ages, all backgrounds, all experiences. If possible, gather both people who know biblical stories very well and people who are complete outsiders to these stories. Do not bring in outsiders to the story in order to trick them into "becoming Christians." Quite the contrary: bring in outsiders in order to learn things from them about your own biblical stories. As you will discover, there are things about biblical stories that outsiders see better than do insiders. Expect to learn a lot.

How large a group should you gather? Five is a good number. So is seven. More than that can make things awkward when you are just starting. Fewer than that can work (I began with a group of three), but it is easier to fall victim to an imagination vapor-lock with smaller groups. If you have five to seven people around, no matter how stuck you get, someone is bound to have a good idea that the group can work with.

Pick a Story

Following are some suggestions for first stories to explore. These are not the only ones that will work. Far from it. You could pick any story at all. There are juicy stories everywhere. These are just a few stories that, in the experience of my team of storytellers, have been consistently juicy and productive. If it helps, each of these suggested stories also appears in the appendix (p. 115) in a form that helps with the next step in this process, the Read-Around. You'll see how that operates in a moment. The translations in each case are my own. You could also use any translation that better suits your needs. The thing to look out for if you pick another translation, however, is the effect of Holy Language (which needs to be written in capital letters). If you find yourself needing to talk in stilted tones (using a vague English accent perhaps) when you read the translation you've chosen, find a different translation. Right away. We are attempting to re-member these stories, to make them part of real human bodies, and no body speaks Holy Language. Trust me on this.

Some possibilities:

Bread in a Boat (Mk. 8:14–21);

And Throw It to the Dogs (Mk. 7:24-30);

The Serpent Was the Cleverest (Gen. 3:1–7).

Warm Up

This part will seem weird.

No, let me rephrase that.

This part will BE weird.

This will be especially true if the group you have gathered is not accustomed to theater games. Do it anyway. I make it a rule for living never to avoid anything simply because it would be weird. There are many good reasons to avoid things—moral grounds, for instance. But to avoid the physical warm-up that is part of this "how-to" guide would be like deciding to follow all of Norm Abrams' advice on the *New Yankee Workshop* except for the part about using a measuring tape carefully. It's hard to do decent carpentry work without using the basic tools.

Physical warm-up is a basic tool for this way of working with biblical stories.

Here are some useful exercises to warm you up. For these exercises, pick a leader who guides the group through the process.

Body Awareness

Sit on the floor (or in a chair if it doesn't work to sit on the floor). Close your eyes and listen to your breathing for four or five breaths. Feel the air rushing in and rushing out. Feel the movement of the muscles that make this happen. Listen to the sound that breathing makes.

Now pay attention to the places your body touches the floor (or chair). Feel your weight and solidity focused where you press against the floor. Feel the floor as it pushes back against you. Continue this awareness exercise for another minute or two. Don't measure this time with a clock.

Body Limberness

Stand in a circle, facing the center. Beginning at the floor, move each joint, each muscle, each limb. Start with your toes, then your ankles, then your knees, each side in turn. Move your hips, spine, shoulders, elbows, hands, and fingers. For each new movement, take sufficient time to concentrate on the limberness, the movement.

Big Body, Little Body

Now that you all are fairly limber and aware, it is time to get really silly. Think of it as creativity. That might work, who knows?

The leader calls out "Big Body" and everyone in the circle stretches up and becomes as big as it is possible to be. Bigness can be achieved in all sorts of ways. Tall is big, but so is wide. Get as big as you can without exploding.

When the leader calls out "Little Body," everyone shrinks to be as small as it is possible to be. Again, there are lots of ways to be small. Learn from each other.

Repeat the process several times until everyone is thoroughly warm and silly. Warm and silly make for good biblical interpretation.

Do a Read-Around

Sit in a circle. Make the circle small enough and tight enough that everyone can see everyone, hear everyone, and touch everyone. Make sure everyone has a copy of the story you have chosen for a Read-Around: it doesn't work so well if people have to pass the written text back and forth. Make sure everyone notices the way the text is arranged in line fragments. Decide who starts the Read-Around. That person reads a single line fragment, followed by the next person around the circle, followed by the next and the next, and so on.

Now you are going to do laps. You are going to read through the story, line fragment by line fragment, person by person, around and around the circle. Go through the story at least three times before you stop. On the first lap, each person reads her line as quickly as possible, beginning if possible before the previous reader has finished her last word. On the first lap you want speed, not emoting. On the second lap, ask each person to read her line fragment with some large, and probably random, emotion. It does not matter if the emotion flows from what the previous reader attempted or not. It does not matter if the emotional reading makes any sense at all. It is often better and more productive if it does not. On this lap you want huge eruptions, motivated or not. And you want this reading to go quickly.

On the third lap, ask everyone to try to link her emotion (still huge and overblown) to something that the people before her in the circle seem to have been trying. Again, it doesn't matter if the link is altogether successful or if the emotion theme people are trying makes very much sense. Again, strange attempts are sometimes better and more enlightening than normal ones.

What-Did-You-Hear-What-Did-You-Notice?

After three (usually chaotic) laps, stop and ask what people have heard and noticed. Did any of the odd emoting make surprising sense? Did any of the line fragments that followed each other turn into arguments (whether or not the story was about an argument)? Did any of the racing line fragments turn into a love story? A detective story? A slumber party? In all of this you are after the rhythms and surprises of the language. You are looking to destabilize usual readings of the story. If your experience is like my experience with my team of storytellers, you will often find fascinating tensions, fractures, and healings (not always in that order) hiding behind the curtains of "normal" readings of "normal" stories.

You are looking for exactly these sparks and tensions. You may not be sure that they mean anything. Often they do not. But sometimes they do indeed mean something, and sometimes it is something rather significant, and then you have something exciting to explore. Sometimes it takes a few more laps before anything suggests itself.

Attempt Some First Embodiments

Once you have identified interesting (if odd) sparks and tensions, make some first attempts at embodying them. This is where the silliness of the warm-up comes in handy. What comes next will often seem strange or silly.

If a certain stretch of the story sounded like a love story (for whatever reason), play that stretch (and sometimes the entire story) as a love story. Or as a detective story, or as whatever occurs to someone in the group.

It works best to attempt these first experimental tellings in pairs. Ask two courageous members of the company to stand in front of the group and try something. The instructions are exactly that vague. When I'm working with my team of storytellers, we do not even usually divide up the lines between the two players on the first attempt. Rather, we let them fight it out as they attempt to play the love story (or whatever) for the group. Try working this way. If you find that it works better to decide who says what before you begin, do that, at least for now.

The important thing to keep in mind at this point is that you are telling the story, not acting it out. Don't divide the parts so that one person is the narrator and the others are the characters. At least don't do that yet. You may decide later on that such a division is the most productive way to work with the story at hand, but don't start there.

The reasons for this suggestion are a little complicated, but they mostly come down to a distillation of several years of experience and exploration. It just works better if you don't divide the scenes into character and narrator parts. As I said, you are telling the story, not acting it out. You can and might choose to rework the story into a dramatic scene, but that would require a complete restructuring of the scene. For now, stick with storytelling, which means that everybody says the "she said" and "he said" lines, and everybody speaks the stage directions aloud as part of her role. This will seem odd to start with, and if some of your group have experience in acting, they will surely ask if they can just omit the "she said" lines. Just say no.

One result of treating the text as a storytelling text that is shared by two (or more) players is that the tensions in the text will pop into view more quickly and clearly. Sometimes, maybe even most times, these tensions will indeed be between two of the characters in the scene. In such a case, if you have two players working on the scene you can assign one to each side. Continue to speak the "she said" lines.

But sometimes you will discover that it appears, at least to the group on the day you are working, that the lines of tension, the fractures, are more complicated than that. Sometimes the fault lines run not between characters but through them. Sometimes it sounds for all the world as if characters are, in fact, arguing with themselves as much as they are arguing with each other. For instance, in the gospel of Luke Jesus says one time, "Anyone who is not against us is for us," and another time, "Anyone who is not with us is against us." Yes, you could explain this away (always a bad idea) by manufacturing reasons that would demonstrate once and for all that Jesus is perfectly unified, perfectly calm, and perfectly correct. That is the usual response to such surprises. Avoid the usual; distrust the customary. You can always go back to the "standard issue" ways of playing and understanding such scenes, but don't start there. Always trust such discoveries of tensions and fault lines, even if you decide later that you were wrong. And always play such discoveries as scenes that embody the tensions. Sometimes you will discover something basic and important about an argument that helped shape the earliest Christian movement, an argument that just might help make sense of Christian faith in the contemporary world.

When the first pair finishes experimenting with the scene, the rest of the group responds by reporting what they noticed. What worked? What could be sharper? And then the two play the scene again. And again. And again.

Process is very important at this point. You are doing many things at once, and it matters that you be clear about that. You are beginning to explore the inner structure of the story you have chosen. You are beginning to learn to work together as a team. You are beginning to learn to trust each other (and the story) physically.

And what matters most of all is that you are *beginning*. Your first attempts to embody the text will very likely yield not too much: a nervous laugh or two, a strange and largely unworkable skit-like device that you can't imagine allowing any human being on this planet (or any other) ever to see. And maybe not much more.

If you focus on what you *have not* accomplished, you will never get anywhere. Focus on what you have accomplished. Here's a hint as to what that might have been: you have *begun*. You have begun to explore, to work together, and to trust. And remember, you are beginning to trust not only each other, but also the text. This trust is in itself a huge accomplishment. So much biblical interpretation seems to proceed from the notion that the Bible must be protected somehow, protected at any cost. The result is that interpreters make mighty efforts to guarantee that their interpretation will say, in the end, exactly what everyone in the room already thought it would say.

My question is a simple one, and somewhat rude, I guess. If the end result has to agree with what everyone already thinks, why go through the effort of interpreting the story in the first place? Why not just do a focus-group, take a poll, sound out the group, and take the mishmash that results as the meaning of the story you are exploring?

I think that proper biblical interpretation ought to surprise everyone, including the interpreter. I think that a biblical story that is told well will often stun its audience. And, most important of all, I am quite confident that the Bible will stand up to our strangest attempts to tell its stories. The Bible has survived the snores that have greeted dull preaching and the cheers that have greeted dangerous enthusiasms through all these centuries. I would imagine that you can trust it to survive your efforts to tell its stories, how ever odd or awkward those efforts will be at times. You have begun to trust. That is a huge accomplishment.

As you finish your first attempts to work with biblical stories in this odd and new way, remember also that the trust you are developing is indeed physical. As you learn to link the words of the story to your actions and reactions, you will discover the fascinating link between this kind of re-membering (which is the opposite of dis-membering) and remembering, what Tom Boomershine calls "learning by heart." This physical learning of the text will bear fruit in good time. Wait for it. For now, remember (re-member?) the quotation that began this chapter. Leslie Marmon Silko, a writer with a Laguna Pueblo background, wrote "You don't have anything, if you don't have the stories." When you have worked through this process of re-membering, embodying, biblical stories, you will indeed have them.

The question is: will the stories have you?

Homework

Yes, there is homework that goes with the "how-to" portions of this book. I hesitate to use the word, knowing that there are people who make it a moral point to refuse to do homework. This is different.

Go to the movies. Any movie will do, at least almost any movie. Watch the bodies, watch the ways the words are embedded in the bodies. Watch the ways the story is embodied, re-membered.

This works even better if you can go to the theater to see a play. Even amateur productions will show you something useful about embodiment, but skilled actors in a polished production will show you much more. The advantage of the theater over the movies is that you can see whole bodies interacting with each other, not just the close-ups of faces that make up so much of cinematography. Watch the hands, watch the feet, watch the knees, watch the whole body.

Something else you should do: recall carefully the cartoons and TV shows you watched as a child. Remember them as thoroughly as you can. Now find a child and watch TV with her for a few days. What shows hold and shape her interest? What is the narrative structure of those shows? What was the narrative structure of the shows you watched? Spend some time reflecting on how these narrative structures have shaped the world you live in.

Suggested Reading

Eco, Umberto. *Six Walks in the Fictional Woods.* Cambridge: Harvard University Press, 1984.

Ende, Michael. *The Neverending Story.* Garden City, N.Y.: Doubleday, 1983.

Levy, Shimon. *The Bible as Theatre.* Brighton, England: Sussex Academic Press, 2000.

Lewis, C. S. *Essays Presented to Charles Williams.* Grand Rapids: Eerdmans, 1966, especially the essay "On Fairy Stories," by J. R. R. Tolkien.

2

Taking Place . . . Taking Up Space

To welcome the Other is to put in question my freedom.

—Emmanuel Levinas

[E]verything a person does in their life can be reduced to two essential actions: "to pull" and "to push." We do nothing else! . . . everything brings us back to pull/push.

—Jacques Lecoq

The face resists possession, resists my powers.

—Emmanuel Levinas

Tout bouge.

—Jacques Lecoq

PART ONE: WHY TO TAKE UP SPACE

Your first task as a reader of this chapter will be to figure out what the writings of these two Frenchmen—one a philosopher, the other a man of the theater—have to do with each other. If your first thought, having read the quotations, is "not much," you have begun well. Now let's go further.

The Pull and the Push

The last quotation from Jacques Lecoq, the founder of the International School of Mime and Theatre, is the basic idea that gives life to a whole school of dramatic performance. Two words, but they have enormous significance and power. But they're in French. If your French is good, that's no problem. But if the last time you saw your French, it was in high school, in the *bibliotheque,* and it was salivating over a plate of *veau aux épinards,* it won't be particularly helpful to know that the words *tout bouge* could be so significant. What do they mean?

The words are often translated as "Everything moves." That is a workable translation. Solid enough. Reliable. And it names something important about the kind of theater, the kind of dramatic practice, that Lecoq taught, centered as it was (and as it is in the work of his collaborators and students in places like the Theatre de la Jeune Lune in Minneapolis, Minnesota) in movement studies.

The translation, "everything moves," is good and workable, but it misses the force of the word, I think.

Translation is a funny business. Words do not simply move back and forth across linguistic borders, they are not simply traded at a regular rate of exchange. Though words surely name things, and though different languages surely name the same things, that does not necessarily mean that the work of translation is finished when two languages bump into an object and trade their words for the object. Even the simplest of names brings with it a crowd of associations and implications, and any proper translation works also to consider how this crowd affects the words one ultimately chooses as a translation. Words are not simply so much roughage. The crowd of associations and implications add flavors that are essential to the meaning of a word.[1]

A place to observe the force of associations and implications in translation (and a useful help if your French is not what it used to be, or never was) can be found in the operation of machine translators found on the Worldwide Web. To see how complicated translation can be, even of a fairly simple bit of language, pick a poem you find interesting (one fascinating piece to try this with is Rilke's "The Panther") and run it back and forth through a machine translator: German to English, English to German, German to English, and so on. Because of the assumptions about associations and implications that are built into machine translators, the poem will migrate in meaning toward some rather surprising readings. Words are not simply words, and machine translation makes this clear.

So what happens if you run "Tout bouge" through several Web-based translators? First, you will discover that several such sites do, indeed, translate it as "Everything (or All) moves." So far, so ordinary. More sites, however, prefer as a translation the nonsentence "Any bulge." This is, again, clearly within the set of possible meanings for these words, though it makes little sense.

It may make little sense, but that little sense is useful sense. "Move" in English is a word without precision or direction. It applies to things random and things purposeful, to everything from Brownian movement (random vibration) to a move on a chess board, and to a great many other things as well. The word could be anything.

"Bulge," however, has a different flavor. Bulges are neither random nor directionless. A bulge is pushed out of something. Even when the word is used to describe a simple, fixed geographic feature (a bulging hill, for instance), the metaphor implies force and directed movement. So perhaps we ought to try to translate Lecoq's famous dictum as "Everything bulges." Or perhaps not, at least not yet.

One of the machine translators offered a particularly interesting reading of the sentence. "Tout bouge," it suggested, should be read as "All budges." This seems more in line with what Lecoq had in mind. A budge is like a bulge in that it has direction and force. But a budge asserts its own particular meaning when it brings into the sentence the implication of another (an Other?)[2] who feels the force of the budge and who might budge back in return. Now, I think, we have caught Lecoq's force. The movement[3] on which he focuses is not the random, or even self-directed movement of an atomized self drifting without impingement.[4] The movement Lecoq focuses on is the pull/push of real life. For a scene on stage to work, it must respect this real life pulling and pushing. Actors aiming to engage an audience will study dramatic texts to discover the pull/push of real life as it operates between the characters in a scene, and they will develop ways of playing the scene that show real pushes and real pulls. The laws of real life (and dramatic) movement make it clear that any push pushes something, or someone, and any pull exerts a real tug. And the tug pulls on another (an Other).

And with the Other we finally encounter a reason for including words from Emanuel Levinas with those of Jacques Lecoq at the beginning of this chapter. This is what brings Lecoq and Levinas, speaking separately from the theater and from philosophy, into conversation with each other. If "everything budges," if "everything pushes," if "everything impinges," then everything brings us into contact with the other (the Other), then everything draws our eyes to the face of the other whom we pull and push reciprocally.

Why does this matter? A full discussion of this follows. For now, notice that the reality of pulling and pushing an Other who resists your powers makes it very clear that any understanding of life that imagines a world in which there is one script (mine) and one originator of movement (me) will be attended by the rudest of surprises, on stage and off. These rude surprises lead rookies in every field to believe that their education really began when they finally entered the "real world" (and thus surprises lead them either to misunderstand their education, or to understand it for the first time). These are the surprises that turn idealists and dreamers into cynics, sometimes of the bitterest sort. And these are the surprises that either create skilled biblical interpreters or finish them off. Bad preaching and teaching, bad biblical interpretation comes, to be sure, from many sources, but it is most distressing when bad interpretation is the result of shattered naïveté, the result of an interpreter not knowing (somehow!) that life is pull and push. But we have all heard, and produced interpretations of such marvelous abstraction that they could only live in the strictest vacuum created by a naïve ideology and spirituality.

Why does this matter? It matters because story analysis gets much further when it begins with a careful look at the physical reality of the world of the story, with an attentive examination, first, of the pull and push within the story, and then of the pull and push between the story and the interpreter. In the International School of Mime and Theatre, Jacques Lecoq rooted textual analysis in movement analysis.

> As a first stage, we make gestures as we speak the text, without worrying about its structure. All kinds of gestures emerge. The purpose of this basic work is to set the text free inside the body, so that the body does not become an obstacle. Once the text

is learned, we strengthen the gestural dynamics, which are performed alone, in silence. Gradually the structure of the text takes shape after its cloudy beginnings.

Next we work on improving the quality of the gestures, then, in small 'domes,' made up of five to seven students standing in a circle, we look for the most appropriate gestures while speaking in chorus. One student, chosen as the best mimer of his group, stands in the centre and conducts the words of the chorus, which the others speak without moving. Working from gestures to immobility, the text is learned.[5]

Now, the goal of Lecoq's work is clearly different from the goal of most interpreters. Lecoq is training people for the theater; he is aiming at the performance of a play. This makes his work different even from the work of a storyteller, perhaps, and surely different from the work of most biblical interpreters. But notice that, for all the real differences, there are also some important similarities here. Lecoq aims to know the text, to learn it, and this surely means more than to simply commit it to memory. In particular, he aims to discover the structure of the text. In this, his work overlaps with biblical work of all eras, with structuralist and poststructuralist just as surely as with traditionalist readings of all sorts. But notice that this structure is discovered, not in static outlines, but in the pull/push of the text. Notice that for the text to "take place" (a marvelous metaphor), it must be brought to take up space, and it does that by pulling and pushing.

And so we begin, in this chapter, as my troupe of storytellers and I begin our analysis of our stories, with an examination of the ways stories take up space. And so we begin, further, by taking up the matter of space as it shapes the ways we participate in stories.

Embodying Stories: This Is My Body

The first step to taking up space is taking up body. The stories we aim to interpret are not about ideas, at least not in some airless and abstract sense. They are stories about real people and real existence, and real people and real existence come only in bodily form. That means, as we understand it, that one only understands biblical stories when one pays careful attention to the bodies in the stories.

In our work we aim to take biblical stories off the page and put them into real life, real bodies. This means, as noted in the first chapter, that we need to pay careful attention to the bodily remembrance of Jesus. The exercise, in our experience, has proved to be a useful reminder of the importance of the doctrine of the Incarnation for Christian theology. The Incarnation has meant, for Christian theology historically, that we have had to struggle to take bodily existence as seriously as God took it in assuming human flesh. That has not been easy. But it has yielded strong results, from historic sacramental theology to contemporary environmental theology, and the effort appears worthwhile. As C. S. Lewis noted somewhere, God must love matter, having made such a great lot of it. If God takes matter seriously, so should we. Matter matters, so to speak.

So what body does Jesus have in the stories we are interpreting? If the interpreters are storytellers, Jesus will end up speaking through the body of one of the company, somehow. Part of honoring the Incarnation involves working hard to honor the body of Jesus, the first-century Jew. That means that any responsible interpretive work will, of necessity, involve careful investigation of the historical and cultural world of Jews in the first century of the Common Era. Everything from clothing to possible political aspirations to the probable language(s) of everyday life will require research as part of the effort to honor the historical particularity of the embodiment of Jesus.[6]

But another part of honoring Jesus' historical particularity, and surely part of exploring it, involves taking seriously the embodiments that are possible within the troupe of available players. It involves honoring their effort to embody the words and actions of the character as words and actions of a real human being, with the usual capabilities and incapabilities. The character, Jesus, changes when he is embodied by a young man or an old man, or by a woman, young or old. His healings have an extra bite when they are performed by a person with cerebral palsy. His words sound different when they come out of a Native American mouth than they do when spoken by a European American, and different still when spoken by someone of African descent, whether from America or not. Unless a member of the troupe of storytellers just happens to be a cryogenically frozen and now revived Jewish male from the first century of the Common Era, Jesus will have to be played by actors, each of whom brings something different to the part. Each of these differences, each of these particular consequences of embodiment, is crucial as part of the effort to honor the particular reality of human life. Too much biblical interpretation proceeds as if Jesus were an idea, not a person. Such notions were rejected as heretical early in the life of the Christian movement, but they live on in every Christian community I have ever been part of. In our experience as storytellers, it takes real effort to prevent the character Jesus from evaporating into some sort of spiritual haze, to hold ourselves to playing him as a person, a body. Here, too, matter matters.

To interpret these stories, and especially to tell them, we will also have to find a way to embody demons. For some interpreters this will pose no great problems. I have friends and colleagues who live in Africa for whom demons are active characters in the everyday world. I do not live in such a world. My friends and colleagues see this as a distinct liability, a possibly harmful constriction imposed by the world I live in. They may well be correct. But I was raised to take the world seriously, and that has meant that I have been brought up to seek physical, chemical, and biological causes for the behaviors I encounter in myself and others. I do not begin (or end) by speculating about demons when I encounter things that I cannot explain. I do not see demons and I do not expect to start seeing them.

Except when I read biblical narrative. In that world they are on every other page, and a storyteller will necessarily have to find a way to embody them. Persuasively.

That's the hard part. Anybody can cook up a cheesy stereotyped version of a cartoon demon. If need be, you could even dig up a pitchfork and pointy tail.

Or, to go the other way, anybody could continue the interpretive tradition of reading demons as misnamed psychological conditions. In my reading, such solutions solve nothing and miss most of the force of the story. As soon as the demoniac that Jesus encounters is "actually" a person with schizophrenia, their dialog becomes the stuff only of delusion. "What's all this to you and to me, Jesus Netzer,"[7] says the victim of a chemical imbalance. As soon as my interpretive framework requires me to condescend to the story, I become unable to read the story any longer, or even to see it. Interpretation becomes a matter of making excuses for a text that couldn't be expected to know any better. I do not expect great things of interpretation that begins with condescension.

But how does one embody a demon? What voice would work? What posture? What movements? In our work, because we aim to provoke the gospel, these questions remain questions. We have found a rotating set of provisional answers, but the responsibility to embody the text has precluded our developing a stable, final answer. Maybe this would be easier in Africa. I do not know.

And we have to embody the disciples. They have posed particularly interesting challenges. There is, for instance, Peter, that rock of a disciple,[8] who, on the Mountain of Transfiguration, offers to make tents for dead people. Or there are James and John, who hear Jesus predict his suffering and death and respond with the following scene from Mark 10:35–40:

> Then James and John walked up to him
>> (they're the two sons of Zebedee),
>> they walked up and said:
>> Teacher? Okay: whatever we ask, you have to do it, okay?.
> He said to them,
>> What do you want me to do for you?
> They said to him:
>> Okay:
>> Give us this:
>>> in your glory
>>> one of us sits on your right,
>>> one of us on your left,
>>> okay?
> Jesus said to them:
>> You don't know what you are asking.
>>> Are you able to drink the cup that I drink?
>>> Or the baptism I undergo, are you able to take that, too?
> They said to him:
>> We can do that, no problem.
> Jesus said to them:
>> The cup I drink, you will drink.
>> The baptism I undergo, you will undergo.
>> But sitting at my right or my left?
>>> That isn't mine to give.
>>> It belongs to those for whom it was prepared.

And just in case you still retain any positive feeling for discipleship as practiced by John, he disgraces himself yet again in Mark 9:38–40:

John said to him:
    Teacher, we saw someone,
        (in your name!)
casting out demons and we tried to stop him.
    He was not following you.
Jesus said:
    Don't try to stop him.
    There isn't anyone
who will do a deed of power
    upon my name
and then be able quickly to speak evil of me.
    Anyone who is not against us is for us.

This is an odd way to portray Jesus' closest followers, his disciples, odd and strikingly negative. Stranger still because the Greek word for "disciple" means "learner." Time after time in Mark the learners demonstrate that they are incapable of learning anything. This is such an odd portrayal of the disciples that serious scholars have argued that the gospel was written, in part, to discredit the disciples as leaders and models in the ancient church. Whether that is true or not, the picture is odd, negative, and frequently hilarious.

And the question is how to embody these odd characters. The traditional, standard-form treatment found in most churches doesn't begin to touch the oddity of the disciples. Christians know, at least since Dietrich Bonhoeffer's *Cost of Discipleship*, that discipleship is a serious, costly business, and so the disciples are understood, and portrayed, to be serious people who are awed by their circumstances. This leaves the scenes with too much left disembodied. James and John do not seem likely to be able to figure out that they ought to join the resistance against Hitler. In any case, they seem more interested in getting good seats than in Bonhoeffer's call to "come and die." If these disciples are to be re-membered and embodied adequately, then other, stranger bodies are needed.

Once when my storytellers and I were working on the problem of how to embody these strange disciples, a member of the troupe remarked that sometimes the disciples look so strange that it seems that their names should be Peter, James, and John, Curly, Larry, and Moe. Out of that rather surprising suggestion came the following scene depicting the story in Mark 8:14–21, which we have come to call "Knuckleheads."

Curly

They had forgot to bring bread.
    They had only one loaf with them in the boat.

Moe

    Jesus was commanding them:
        Watch out.
        Beware of the leaven of the Pharisees
            and the leaven of Herod.

Larry

    They were saying to each other:
    It's because we don't have any bread.

Moe

    When he realized what they were doing,
        he says to them:
            Why are you saying:
                It's because we don't have any bread?
            Don't you get it?
            Do you really not understand?
                How thick are your skulls, anyway?
                    You have eyes, and you can't see?
                    Ears you have, but you can't hear?
            Nobody remembers?
            When I broke five loaves for 5000 people,
                how many baskets of leftovers did you pick up?

Larry

        They say to him:
            Twelve.

Moe

> And the seven loaves for the 4000?
> How many baskets of leftovers did you pick up?

Curly

> They say:
> Seven.

Moe

> He kept saying to them:
> You don't get it yet, do you?

These are, to be sure, strange bodies, maybe too strange. But notice that the lines work coming out of those too strange bodies. Curly, Larry, and Moe could indeed do this scene as a Stooges routine. I do not hope ever to see the gospel of Mark played by the Three Stooges, but it is fascinating to note that these bodies, at least, catch the oddity of the way Mark portrays Jesus' closest followers.

Taking Up Space

And so we take up bodies, and so we also take up space, or rather, the matter of space.

What might that mean? We begin by noticing something exceedingly simple. On a page everything is compressed and flattened. Reading, as noted in the first chapter, may blow things up off the page, projecting the story into imaginary life in all its dimensions, but printing takes place on flat surfaces that can be closed between covers. That means that, for all the magic, books will always be different from real life, because in real life, when things really happen, when they take place, they take up space. That means that books, stories, will always relate to real life the way topographical maps relate to real mountains, hills, valleys, rivers, and lakes.

And that means that responsible interpreters have to look carefully for the ways that the story they are reading and telling takes place. They have to look for the traces of space preserved on the page, and they have to pay exquisite attention to those traces of space. Those traces are what allow an interpreter to reconstitute the world of the text, to transform the topographical lines, thoroughly abstract, into real space, into real life with all its pull and push.

When you pay exquisite attention to the preserved traces of space, most of what you find is pretty basic. Stories are littered with spatial references, but most of them are things like here and there, in and out, up and down. Following Lecoq's lead, a responsible interpreter recognizes these simple, basic spatial dimensions as crucial to the story and its structure. They create the space in which the story and its characters pull and push, the only things we do.

Following Lecoq's lead, an interpreter finds (as Lecoq would expect) that the simple spatial dimensions of the story also reveal the structure of the story. In Mark's story, events happen in Galilee or Jerusalem, a here/there structure that makes a great deal of difference for the way Mark tells his story. In Mark's story, Jesus is either in a house, or out of the house, and this in/out structure has been tracked by interpreters who have long recognized that it also is a structuring member of the story.

And there is a scene at the beginning of Mark's gospel (Mk. 1:9–12) that brings together all three of these spatial dimensions in a single episode.

It happened in those days:
    Jesus came from Nazareth of Galilee
        and was baptized in the Jordan by John.
    He is coming up out of the water
        and BANG he sees the heavens being torn apart
            and the spirit,
                like a pigeon,
        coming down into him.
    A voice came out of the heavens:
        You are my son, the beloved.
            With you I am well pleased.
    Then BANG the spirit threw him out into the wilderness.

This scene is so important in Mark's story that you cannot make effective sense of the story unless you notice it, unless you pay exquisite attention to it. You hear the reference to Galilee, where Jesus was before he came to the Jordan near Jerusalem. He was *there*, now he's *here*. You hear the reference to John baptizing Jesus in the Jordan. And you see him coming *up* out of the water, and see him looking further *up*, all the way to the dome of the heavens, which is then ripped apart to open up the space of the story all the way to infinity. And out of infinity comes the spirit by which God gave life to creation, out of infinity comes God's voice, which spoke and brought all things into being, made them what they are. The spirit comes *down* like a pigeon, and goes *into* him.

These spatial references establish the space of the story, the world in which the pull/push of life takes place. And once the space of the story has been opened all the way to the infinite, a voice speaks. Presumably it is God who speaks and makes Jesus what he is in Mark's whole story: God's son, the beloved, which is to say, in this story Jesus is the messiah, the king. This is not the last time we will hear God's voice in this story. This will be explored more fully at another time. For now just notice the way this scene takes place.

Tout Bouge: Everything Budges

There is another kind of spatial relation in Mark's story that we need to catch. Listen to this story from Mark 5:25–34. Watch for how it takes up space, how it takes place. Imagine the space.

A woman came,
    a woman twelve years in a river of blood,
        twelve years having suffered many things
        under many healers,
    a woman who had exhausted all her property,
        all her substance,
        after twelve years she had improved not at all,
            in fact, her condition had grown worse.
A woman came into the area,
    came because she had heard about Jesus.
This woman came into the crowd behind Jesus
    and touched his clothing.
    She was saying:
        even if I only touch the hem of his garment,
            I will be rescued.
BANG the spring of her blood was dried up
    and she knew in her body
    that she was healed from her scourge.

BANG Jesus knew in himself
    that power had gone out from him.
Turning and turning, around in the crowd,
    he kept saying:
        Who touched my clothing?
    His disciples were saying to him:
        You can see the crowd crushing you
        and you say: Who touched me?
He kept looking around
    to find the woman who had done this.
The woman,
    afraid and trembling,
knew what had happened to her.
The woman came and fell down before him.
She told him the whole truth.
He said to her:
    Daughter, your faithfulness has saved you.
    Depart in peace
and be healed from your scourge.

Did you notice the space? This is a simple story, a healing story, which makes it a central story in Mark's gospel. In Mark's story, Jesus is a healer, God's agent to restore wholeness to the creation. But did you notice how space shapes this simple, central story? She comes up behind him. She touches him. She falls at his feet. And then something decisive happens to the space they have all been moving through. Jesus and the woman meet face to face. Now space has a tense connectedness. Now real life begins, at least according to Emmanuel Levinas. Now Jesus sees "the gleam of transcendence in the face of the Other."[9] Now Jesus is drawn into the encounter that is the core of ethics.[10] Now Jesus' freedom is "put in question."[11]

Of course, there are not only two faces in this scene. The scene takes place in a crowd, and opening the space wider changes both the scene and the ethical relation. Now Jesus encounters not just the face of the woman who touches him but also the faces of the crowd in which he dithers, looking for "the woman who had done this." What was originally a simple healing story has become, because we have taken up the space in which the story takes place, a much more complicated thing. When you open up the space, you get another view, a view that might well change your reaction to the simple scene we first looked at.

The story becomes even more complicated if you open the space even wider. This is necessary as part of the effort to understand this scene because when this healing takes place, Jesus is on his way from here to there, to a house in which a little girl is dying. When Jesus finishes his "turning and turning around in the crowd," when he encounters the woman face to face, when he finishes this embedded scene, the space of the story is forced open by what happens next (Mk 5:35).

> While he was still speaking
> they came to him from the leader of the synagogue:
>> Your daughter has died, they said,
>> why bother the teacher any longer?

When you open up the space, you see an oddity that makes considerable difference. The little girl died while the surgeon wandered aimlessly in the crowd, chasing wild geese, perhaps.

Now, you probably know that when Jesus arrives at the girl's house he raises her from the dead. That matters. But stay here just for a second. If space is constituted in the tense, connected space between faces, and if real life begins in that tense space, then what happens to that space when the woman hears that a little girl had died while Jesus was turning and turning around in the crowd, looking for her? Imagine the woman's face when she heard *that* news. Now imagine what this simple story would sound like if it were told by the woman, on the spot, immediately after she heard that the little girl had died. That does indeed make a difference.

And it makes for an odd picture of Jesus, not the last one in Mark's odd little gospel.

What do we know so far? Mark seems to tell his stories (or at least one of them) so that they have a germ at the center of them, in this case the face-to-face encounter between the woman and Jesus. There is embedded in the story, however, a wider space, and this wider space gives a different view, a different perspective. There is in the story an even wider perspective, one that changes things considerably. This final, widest view embodies a fairly odd picture of Jesus and his activities.

A Woman Heard About Him

Now we turn our attention to another scene, another place, another woman, another daughter. Now we will examine another face-to-face encounter, from Mark 7:24–26.

> He went up from there,
>   away into the region of Tyre.
> He went into a house,
>   he wanted no one to know.
>   There was no hiding him.
> A woman heard about him,
>   a woman whose daughter had an unclean spirit.
>   She came.
>   She fell at his feet.
>   The woman was a Gentile,
>   Syrophoenician by birth.
>   She asked him to cast the demon out of her daughter.

The Face-to-Face

You might already know what the next line is. In this scene, Jesus is found by a woman who needs his help, a woman who comes to him without any explanation of why or how she heard about him, a woman whose daughter had an unclean spirit. She came to him, she fell at his feet, and Jesus calls her a dog.

You might well know how this story goes from this point. And if you have heard interpretations of this passage, you might also know that people who pick up this passage typically pull the punch on those words of Jesus in order to soften their sting. For instance, A. E. J. Rawlinson says that "the words are probably spoken by our Lord half whimsically, and with a smile: there was that in His manner which encouraged the woman to persist: He wanted to see what she would say if He affected to adopt the conventional Jewish point of view . . ."[12] There are many questions that must be asked of such interpretive efforts, beginning with questions about the notion that Jesus must, of course, stand apart from (and above) the "conventional Jewish point of view," not to mention the anti-Semitic notions that hide behind that bland formulation. But the essential problems become clear as soon as these words are placed in bodies, and the bodies are placed in spatial relation to each other. As soon as this scene is explored as a face-to-face encounter an interpreter, and any audience that is available, sees what is at stake in reading this scene.

Imagine the face-to-face encounter. Imagine in particular the woman's face. She has fallen at Jesus' feet. She has made her request. Imagine she looks up to him, and sees a "whimsical smile" on the face that calls her a dog. There are a great many things that might pass across her face at a moment like that one, but joy and relief are certainly not among them. I can imagine anger. I can imagine resignation. I can imagine astonishment. But I cannot imagine meek acceptance of the violent words, not unless we posit a backstory for the scene that sets the woman up as a customary victim who has learned the posture appropriate for such attacks. And if we imagine her cringing, like a dog used to being whipped, then Jesus' smile becomes even more problematical. Rawlinson was surely trying to preserve an image of Jesus as gentle and good when he painted a whimsical smile on his face, but the outcome is devastating.

Probably the smile comes into the scene also because Rawlinson knows, along with all other ideological interpreters (and that's all of us), that the scene ends with the demon gone from the daughter. The ending is happy and worth smiling about, so interpreters imagine that there ought to be smiles in the middle of the scene, as well. A chief value of taking embodiment seriously, and of taking up the ethical matter of space, a chief value of considering these texts as dramatic texts in the first place, is that interpreters are forced, by the constraints of embodied theater, to allow things to develop in the scenes that are played. The developments that an audience will see on the face of the mother in this scene as she meets Jesus face to face must be taken as real developments that have a real effect on the way the scene is interpreted and played. Jesus cannot smile. If he does the effect is horrible. Or if he smiles at the beginning, he loses that smile somewhere in the middle, when he sees on the face of the other the effect of his "whimsical" words. And if he smiles at the end, it is the smile of someone who learned a lesson he had not intended to learn that day, a rueful, embarrassed smile of the sort that all of us have to wear all too often in the course of learning our ethics face to face.

So What?

In our work with these texts, my storytellers and I have learned to look for moments when the characters in the story meet face to face, for the moments when they create the tense reality that is the real space of life. From these moments we think we discover the real engines that drive the stories that we tell. It is crucial to understand that the task of reading, telling, and interpreting these stories requires re-membering of the characters, particularly Jesus, requires making Jesus present in the telling of the story. But it is equally important that interpreters take seriously the responsibility to re-member the other characters, the other bodies, the other faces in the story. When these other characters are also re-membered, when the tense space between them is honored and explored, then the scenes we study develop the potential to actually take place.

But when the space is honored, we find that there are many ways the scene could take place. The confrontation between bodies and faces creates a productive tension that is the drama of the scene, but it does not (normally) create a single way the scene could take place. We normally find ourselves with a whole range of possible ways to let the scene take place, a situation that requires giving careful attention to both the pragmatics and the ethics of interpretation. Pragmatics and ethics run across the same field at this point. Pragmatically, there are easy ways to play a scene and hard ways. The easiest way is always simply to sniff out the dominant (and comfortable) ideological reading and do that reading. But comfort is no great indicator of ethical integrity. It may be necessary, in order to honor the characters in the scene and their interaction, to play the scene in a way that is ideologically uncomfortable. Anything else would treat characters as means to an ideological end, an ethically untenable position, said Immanuel Kant.

Likewise, the pragmatics of performance make it clear that clash plays better than consonance. It may be that some of the possible ways to play a scene will hold an audience's attention, but only at the expense of the integrity of the text.

In both of these cases, a rich interpretive situation is created when space is taken seriously and the gospel is provoked. The complications of that rich situation are the subject of the next chapter. What is clear at this point is something simple: face-to-face encounters, played with integrity, will reveal the risks of treating the scenes in the gospels as simple delivery vehicles for customary ideology.

PART TWO: HOW TO TAKE UP SPACE

Pick a Story

Here's another set of suggested stories to explore. As before, there are many other stories that you could choose. These have the advantage of incorporating interesting spatial aspects, as you will see:

He's Coming Up Out of the Water (Mk. 1:4–11);
River of Blood (Mk. 5:21–43);
And Throw It to the Dogs (Mk. 7:24–30);
Sinks-like-a-. . . (Matt. 14:22–33).

Warm Up

This part will still seem weird.

This part will always be weird, at least a little. This part will also always seem like it's the part you could omit. It is not. As I said in the first chapter, physical warm-up is a basic tool for this way of working with biblical stories. This becomes even more true when, as in this session, you begin more explicitly physical play with the stories. Even if all you ever did was stand a couple of players in front of an audience and have them do a "talking heads" telling of the story, still physical warm-up would be crucial. But very little of real life (outside of the evening news) is done by frozen talking heads. Most of life involves whole body interaction, even if the people involved mostly stand still.

So warm up.

You can use the exercises mentioned in the first chapter as a starting place. You probably will always benefit from doing the limberness exercise. Any book of theater games and warm-ups will give you a good set of ideas to work with. The exercises I suggest in this book are sometimes ones that my storytellers and I have invented, but far more often they are simply exercises that we have done, separately and together, in different classes or theater groups over the years. You may even recognize many of them from your own experience.

Here are some useful exercises to warm you up. For these exercises, pick a leader who guides the group through the process.

Body Awareness: (see chapter 1, page 25)
Body Limberness: (see chapter 1, page 26)
Big Body, Little Body: (see chapter 1, page 26)

Mirror Image

Pair up the people in your group and have them stand facing each other. One member of the pair is to be the mirror; the other is to be the person looking into the mirror. Direct them to choose an ordinary activity, something that is part of everyday routine, and perform it in front of the mirror. The mirror is to follow the action exactly.

Ask them to begin slowly. The idea is to make it possible for the mirror to perform her task perfectly. As the players become more skillful, increase the pace and variety of actions. Proceed carefully here. The tendency in most groups is to make this into a contest, an attempt to fool the mirror. While such contests make for good laughs, they are, in fact, counterproductive. The objective is to reward the mirror for paying close, intense attention to the initiator of the action and to form a tight bond between the players. If the exercise develops into a contest, pick one pair of players and direct them to begin playing the exercise in front of the rest of the group, now become an audience. Tell the players (privately) that their objective in the exercise is to fool the audience, to perform their task so smoothly that the audience cannot tell who is the mirror and who is the initiator. Tell the audience only that their task is to watch.

A word about audiences: it is important that your group discover that the audience is the most important player in any performance. Every time you assign players to perform in front of the rest of the group, make sure you spend time commissioning the audience members as well. You might even reverse the expected order on such occasions and pick the audience first, leaving the performers as the only ones not chosen to be in the audience. At every opportunity emphasize the active role that an audience plays. This is crucial in the developmental and exploratory stage of your work with biblical stories: you need sharp and attentive eyes on your work as you hunt around inside these strange old stories, eyes that will catch the moments of brilliance that the players themselves will often miss because they are too close to the action. But you also need to train your ensemble to honor their audiences, to think of them as cocreators of the interpretations they are developing. This will make for better performances. Even more important, it will train your ensemble to listen carefully to the questions audiences will ask them, it will prepare them to understand that questions, even objections, are occasions to explore the stories even further.

When the pair has finished the mirror performance, ask the audience what they saw, what they noticed. These are the questions you will always ask. You are not after evaluating and judging. You want only to gather what they have noticed. With judging comes (too often) attack, or at least the establishing of a pecking order. Such hierarchies serve no useful purpose in your work. They only make people more likely to freeze up in front of audiences. This is not an outcome you are seeking.

Encourage noticing of fine detail, interesting moments. When the noticing has proceeded a good while, ask the audience who was playing the part of the mirror, and who the initiator. Your aim at this point is not to determine if the audience was fooled completely the whole time. No audience ever will be fooled the whole time. Your aim is to hunt for moments in which the actors watched each other so attentively that the audience was fooled, even if only for a brief moment. Explore with the audience what it was that made these moments (even if they lasted only a nanosecond) so effective.

Now ask the group to pair up again and perform the exercise one more time. This time they should choose actions that require whole body involvement. Again, start slowly. Emphasize that the objective is to draw the audience so deeply into the performance that they cannot tell who is the mirror and who is the initiator.

This exercise will strengthen the noticing skills of your players, their ability to perform the role of an audience. This will be crucial as you develop into an interpretive team. The exercise will also tighten the bonds between your players, which is also crucial to the strengthening of your shared interpretive work. But there is another important goal of this exercise, one that will take time to develop. This exercise will increase the players' awareness of the physicality of the space between them as they play the scenes you are beginning to develop. As they become increasingly aware of the ways bodies interact physically, even without touching, they will move away from playing biblical stories as verbal pieces needing only talking heads. They will move toward discovering the physical interaction that is at the core of all human life. They will discover the truth of what Jacques Lecoq said at the beginning of this chapter: "[E]verything a person does in their life can be reduced to two essential actions: 'to pull' and 'to push.' We do nothing else!"

As always, warm up until everyone is thoroughly warm and silly.

Do a Read-Around

This is also a permanent feature of this kind of work. As you do more and more Read-Arounds, the people in your group will get better and better at them. There will still be many times when nothing much happens other than you get the text of the story out into the air. That is a necessary outcome in any case, and is sufficient reason for doing a Read-Around. But as people get more accustomed to the practice and more comfortable around each other, they will take bigger risks. Out of bigger risks come better results. The sparks and tensions will reveal more. The physical emotion will open the text wider, which always makes exploration easier.

Sit in a circle as you did last time and again do three laps, aiming at bigger and bigger emotions and reactions. Always complete a Read-Around by exploring what has been heard, seen, and noticed.

Do a "Gesture-Around"

This is an extension of the Read-Around suggested by the work of Jacques Lecoq, described earlier in this chapter. Here is his description of the process:

> As a first stage, we make gestures as we speak the text, without worrying about its structure. All kinds of gestures emerge. The purpose of this basic work is to set the text free inside the body, so that the body does not become an obstacle. Once the text is learned, we strengthen the gestural dynamics, which are performed alone, in silence. Gradually the structure of the text takes shape after its cloudy beginnings.
>
> Next we work on improving the quality of the gestures, then, in small "domes," made up of five to seven students standing in a circle, we look for the most appropriate gestures while speaking in chorus. One student, chosen as the best mimer of his

group, stands in the centre and conducts the words of the chorus, which the others speak without moving. Working from gestures to immobility, the text is learned.[13]

This will require practice and repetition. No group will be instantly able to do this exercise effectively. Start slowly and gently. Do a few laps. Gather what people have noticed. Plan to do the exercise again in the future, and expect that it will be more productive then.

Stage a Tug-of-War

If Lecoq is correct (and I believe that he is), then the basic actions of a story ought to come down to a tug-of-war. There ought to be a back and forth pull and push in a story (especially a conflict story) that could be pulled out and played in the form of that old children's game. Try it.

The first time you do this, it probably will work best to choose one or two players to speak the text and two players to engage in the tug-of-war implied by their words. Direct the players who will be "tugging" to listen carefully to the story as it is spoken and to let their interaction correspond to the interaction implied by the words and flow of the story. Direct the speakers to tell the story slowly, giving the "tuggers" time to develop their contest. By the way, do not do this with a rope. Direct the tuggers to work with an imaginary rope between them which they will make, through their interaction, physically real for the audience. This is done not just to keep the props simple. Working with a rope that must be made real keeps this from becoming a simple contest of strength. The contest is between the words of the story. In such a contest, a child can out-tug an adult, and it is essential that the players discover that. Working with a rope that must be created also requires that your players pay careful attention to each other, which will strengthen their interactions in this and all other scenes.

Your players will want to decide ahead of time which lines ought to result in the rope being pulled one way or the other. Do not make these decisions ahead of time. You will probably have to make such determinations later, but do not make them before trying the tug-of-war cold. Working without a preexisting plan requires your players to pay attention to each other and to the words of the text. Do you notice a theme developing here?

The first attempt at making the text into a tug-of-war will almost always be a horrible failure. That is a good thing. Ask the tuggers and the speakers to do it again immediately, if possible without talking about it. The second attempt will probably be not much better. Ask the audience what they heard, saw, and noticed. Now the real work begins. If the tuggers ignored the words, the audience will have noticed that. If the tuggers stretched the rope, usually because both players simply wanted to win, the audience will have noticed that as well. If the speakers need to create gaps in their speaking to let the tension develop, the audience will have noticed that, too. And if the tensions in the text require that the lines be divided up differently, the audience will have noticed that. This is the time to think together about how the lines might be divided, since now the whole ensemble has an initial physical sense of the struggle of the text. While this initial physical sense will not be unanimous, it is still good. Make sure that you gather and honor the conflicting ideas people have about how the tension should be structured, about who should win when. Try to play all the suggested possibilities. Remember to ask what people have noticed.

Attempt Some First Embodiments

As you did in the previous session, make some attempts at embodying the sparks and tensions that you have found in your shared exploration. You might want to reread the instructions for "Attempt Some First Embodiments" in the first chapter (page 28). The process is the same and will remain the same throughout your work.

The difference this time is that you are likely now to have discovered something more about the physical tension, even the physical contest implied by the story. Use what you have discovered. Make these tentative embodiments more physical than the ones you tried last time.

This increased physicality might happen all by itself. If so, count yourselves lucky. More likely you will have to explore together ways to make the scenes more physically real. You might, for instance, direct the players who are working on the scene to maintain contact with each other at all times. No matter what they do in the scene, the actors have to be touching each other continually. They will have to invent reasons for this continual touch, of course, but this inventing makes for stronger scenes. You might direct them, alternatively, to use pushes and pulls to punctuate their lines. This will require taking what was learned through the tug-of-war and translating it into something that will work as part of this new scene, played as a love story, a slumber party, a detective story, whatever has suggested itself. This will take several tries and much collaborative noticing from the audience. Do not expect any of this to work brilliantly any time soon. Keep at it. As the group learns to work together in this way, your interpretative work will get stronger and stronger. You just have to wait.

Once the pull and push of the scene is thoroughly established, you might direct the players to play the same scene, with the same physical interaction, but this time with four feet of space between them. The physical interaction has to be the same, but now they cannot touch. This complication will require them to hunt for ways to have a physical effect at a distance. Such physical effect at a distance is a regular part of human life, as anyone knows whose mother caught her eye from across the room. Scolding does not require contact or even words. Together hunt for ways to make such distant physical contact a part of your scenes.

Necessary Multiplicity

Always remember that these exploratory scenes need to be played different ways. This is true when the experiment you are attempting is not working. ("Honest, it sounded promising to play this scene as if Mr. Rogers were trying to order a beer and fried cheese curds in a French restaurant. Who knew that it wouldn't work out?") When the scene you are trying is dying, try something new. That doesn't mean the first attempt was a failure (though sometimes . . .), it just means that the scene hasn't worked *yet*. And it means that you always need to keep things fluid, you always need to try other ways of playing the same scene. This is even more important when an experimental scene has worked very well indeed. At such times it is crucial that you try something else as well, something that isn't yet frozen by its success, something that has a chance to fail magnificently. Magnificent failures are the air you breathe when you work with texts this way.

Actually, it is very likely that *none* of what you have at this point is the sort of thing you could play for an audience. Not yet. At this point, let the story rest a while, long enough to let the yeast you have kneaded in start to work.

Sometimes the yeast works before the next worksession, in which case one of the company will rush in at the beginning of the session and insist on trying something she thought up at 3:00 in the morning. Sometimes a story will rest for a long time. Knead it every now and again, just to see if anything has developed.

Homework

Your homework for this session is a kind of pull/push scavenger hunt. Go find instances of the pull and push that Lecoq says make up our entire lives. You are to watch people as they encounter each other, as they move with and around each other, as they pull and push each other. There are lots of places to find this. Keep your eyes open.

One place you might find especially good instances of pull/push is on sidewalks full of people. Find a place from which you can sit and watch the movement. Notice the ways people negotiate, wordlessly, free passage for themselves through the mass of moving people. Watch the pull and the push that makes all of this happen.

If possible, make a videotape of such a sidewalk over a longer period of time, at least an hour, if you can. Watch the tape with the sound off, so you can concentrate only on the physical negotiation, the physical dance of pull and push that people do with each other without having to speak. You might also try watching the tape on fast forward scan. There is something about fast forward that reveals the physical dance more clearly. It almost looks like a ritual sometimes, which (I suppose) in some ways it is.

Look for moments in the tape, or in your memory of the scene, that are particularly clear moments of pull and push. Examine these moments carefully to isolate the exact negotiated interchange that people do in this dance with strangers. There will be several different kinds of pull/push dances to be observed. Find as many different ones as you can, and try to isolate what characteristics make them different from each other.

In your next worksession with your group, play the tape you have made (or maybe just the isolated moments). Keep the sound turned off. Play the tape on fast forward if that seems to help reveal the key moments in the several different dances.

When you and your group have noticed the various dances, ask some members of the group to perform the dances for the rest of the group.

Play the scenes repeatedly to sharpen the physical pull/push that gives them life. After you have polished the scenes, ask the group what names they would give to each of the various dances you have just worked on.

For more homework, go to the movies or the theater again. Life is hard.

Suggested Reading

Bernasconi, Robert, and Simon Critchley, eds. *Re-Reading Levinas.* Bloomington, Ind.: Indiana University Press, 1991.

Booth, Wayne. *The Company We Keep: An Ethics of Fiction.* Berkeley, Calif.: University of California Press, 1988.

Leitch, Vincent B. *Cultural Criticism, Literary Theory, Poststructuralism.* New York: Columbia, 1992.

Levinas, Emmanuel. *Totality and Infinity.* Pittsburgh: Dusquesne University Press, 1969.

Stevens, Bonnie Klomp, and Larry L. Stewart. *A Guide to Literary Criticism and Research.* Fort Worth, Tex.: Harcourt, Brace, Jovanovich, 1987.

3

How to Make Mistakes

*Shakespeare is so great that it is impossible
to get him right. But we have to change periodically
the ways we get him wrong.*

—T. S. Eliot

*I am fascinated by the difference between the geographic pole
and the magnetic pole. The north pole does not quite coincide with
true north. There is a small angle of difference, and it is lucky that
this angle exists. Error is not just acceptable, it is necessary for the
continuation of life, provided it is not too great. A large error is a
catastrophe, a small error is essential for enhancing existence.
Without error, there is no movement. Death follows.*

—Jacques Lecoq

PART ONE: WHY TO MAKE MISTAKES

You will have noticed by now that this book is a "why-to" and "how-to"
guide. I hope that the dance between "why" and "how" is beginning to
make some basic sense. Now comes this chapter to mess everything up.
This chapter also deploys itself as a "why-to" and "how-to" guide, which
makes sense, given the structure of the whole book.

But this chapter is peculiar, maybe even strange. We are going to talk about how and why to make mistakes. Unless this chapter is heavily ironic (always a possibility), somewhere behind this chapter there must be an assumption that making mistakes is somehow desirable, or at least unavoidable. There is a second, related assumption here, and that is that people who interpret biblical texts would (or should) want to make mistakes. "How-to" books only have a market if there is actually an audience out there that really wants to know how to do the subject of the book.

But does anyone really want to make mistakes? Not likely, at least not at first. Mistakes seem risky, surely unfortunate, and maybe even blameworthy. I would like to argue (persuasively, I hope) that mistakes in interpretation are not only unavoidable, but actually indispensable in the process of interpreting biblical narrative. Wait before you decide if you buy the argument or not.

Tools Required for the Job

The first thing you will need in order to make mistakes is a text, a story to interpret. Not just any story will do. The story needs to be one worth making mistakes about. Thin, grey dishwater stories are of no use. Even if you made magnificent mistakes interpreting such a story (assuming you thought, for some unknown reason, that the exercise was worth your time), no one would care whether you made mistakes or not. For mistakes to be interesting and productive, the story you are interpreting needs to stir a bit of passion. The more passion the better it is, because stories that stir passion draw vigorous audiences. And vigorous audiences make for strong performances, strong interpretations. Especially when you make mistakes.

You need a stirring story for another reason. Thin, watery stories give you no challenge that might lead to a mistake, but a vigorous, energetic story is loaded with enough puzzles, enough surprises, enough booby-traps to require (not just allow) the making of mistakes. If all the details of a story behave themselves, it is hard to work up the energy to read (or ride) the story hard. The story just walks around in a dispirited circle like a pony ride at the county fair. No challenge, no great interest.

But a story that bites back, a story that bucks a little, or sometimes spooks, now that's a story that rewards hard reading. That's a story that's worth making mistakes about. Look at where professional interpreters spend their time and passion. Anyone who is responsible to interpret biblical stories has basic jobs that must be done, and among those basic jobs is the plain, everyday "whitebread" charting of the territory of the story, even the dull parts. And so we all do these basic jobs even when they are dull. But the problems and puzzles are what really draw our attention. Look at the volumes that have been written about the (inserted?) section in the eighth chapter of John, or (better yet) the (missing?) end of the gospel of Mark. There are plenty of parts of Mark and John that (at least seem to) make simple straightforward sense. We don't have to spend much energy on them. We spend our energy on the places that frustrate us when we try to make sense. When a road doesn't go through, interpreters become fascinated. And in such situations we experiment, we take risks, we make mistakes, often good ones.

But there is a second tool needed for this work, something beyond an interesting, challenging text. In order to make productive, profitable mistakes, an interpreter also needs courage. Every interesting, challenging problem that biblical interpreters have found so far has stimulated the generation of safe ideological answers. Look at the end of the gospel of Mark. The story hits a dead end at 16:8, and early interpreters of the story (completers of the story, actually) quickly provided four different kinds of ideologically safe padding to soften the blow. There is the shorter additional ending, the longer additional ending, the combined shorter and longer additional ending, and the longer additional ending with its supplement. Each of these added endings makes good safe sense, and it probably required some kind of courage to take it in hand to add on to an already finished gospel. But as soon as the padded ending is applied, no further interpretive courage is required. All the problems posed by Mark's story are solved, in good order, and the story comes full circle. In fact, if you read and accept the supplemental endings, everything walks slowly around in a well-worn circle, led by an attendant almost as sleepy as the textual horse you are riding.

Even just for interest's sake you need to be courageous enough to generate more interesting readings than the usual ideological pony rides. But there is something larger at stake here, something beyond the alleviation of boredom. What is at stake is the text itself. Any truly powerful text is too important to be surrendered to ideological certainties. Any text that is really worth reading and interpreting needs, even provokes, vigorous and courageous interpretation. That is what T. S. Eliot means when he talks about getting Shakespeare wrong. He means that the text rewards courageous readings that make mistakes. He means that the text must provoke us, and that we must provoke the text. He also means that the text will only remain strong and alive in present-day imagination if interpreters continue to honor it by reading it hard, by making new mistakes that will provoke audiences to continue to rethink the text.

Getting Started

So, if we have a vigorous text, and sufficient courage to read it hard, how do we proceed? The first step is simple. You have to read the text. Aloud. Preferably with several different readers. You have to read the text aloud with several different readers who are good at making interesting mistakes. That is the point of the Read-Arounds you have been doing as part of the "how-to" sections of the first two chapters.

The line fragments that you have been reading are broken as part of an effort to catch the storytelling rhythms of the original language. The lines are also broken so that the story is parceled out to the whole group in small packages. Making sense of the story requires that the players participating in the Read-Around collaborate to make both mistakes and sense.

This collaboration requires, first, that each player in the Read-Around circle read her line as vigorously as possible, exaggerating voice and emotion and impact. At this point, no one is trying to make sense. Everyone is simply trying to crack the text open so the group can see what's inside it, so wild, impossible energy is the order of the day. The bigger the mistakes, the better.

The second requirement of this collaboration is that each player experiment with ways that she might build on the energy developed by the preceding players. As the Read-Around moves into its final laps, the players have to pay increasingly close attention to each other; they have to feed off each other and compound each other's mistakes. That means that the story being read gets bigger, wilder, and more outlandish as it goes around the circle. Sometimes it also becomes completely coherent, wild though it is. More often it remains disjointed; more often the players are only able to create brief moments of coherence that start out of nowhere and end abruptly. Both outcomes have been productive in our experience using Read-Arounds. The first possible outcome sometimes (but rarely) yields the seed of a coherent reading that we will develop fully. The second (quite often) yields some interesting promises of future coherence that are worth trying to develop and extend. Both outcomes are beneficial, and even results that seem utterly unusable will lead you to notice lines, fragments, words, or themes that you will not have heard before, even in texts that you know very well indeed. This is exactly what you are after.

With a group of practiced performers, the Read-Around can be wild, even hilarious, sometimes bizarre. Readings are hinted at that will never be developed, never *should* be developed. Some things that come up in such Read-Arounds are too strange, even for us. With the groups that come to our workshops, the Read-Arounds tend to be tamer, more conventional, but even in these more customary readings people hear and feel things that they had never noticed before. Such discoveries and provocations are the beginning of the process of making productive mistakes.

Before we begin exploring these discoveries, before we begin making purposeful mistakes (especially with workshop groups), we make sure to note that everyone in the room knows what the story is supposed to mean, what we have always heard that it means. We know what the story customarily means because the typical workshop group has considerable experience inside a faith community that reads and interprets the text we are playing with. In our little group of storytellers alone we have over two hundred years of experience in church and Sunday school. In those two centuries of enculturation we have learned very well what the stories are supposed to mean. We know the customary ideology, and may very well choose, interpretively, to return to it when we have finished making mistakes. It is important to begin with such an acknowledging of what we do indeed know, because a group, especially a workshop group that will be linked together only for a short time, needs to understand that the process of playing with a text, of making mistakes with it, can only profitably proceed in the context of granting a kind of provisional trust to the regular way of reading the text.[1] By stipulating ahead of time that we all, as a group, know and (at least to some extent) trust the usual stable readings of the stories we will be exploring and provoking, we also begin the process of actively trusting each other as we look for ways to make mistakes with the stories.

We are, after all, not simply trying to make mistakes randomly and for no purpose. In all sorts of areas of life it is better to make purposeful mistakes than to attempt a sort of too-tidy perfection. For instance, in my family we are wilderness canoeists. Imagine you are navigating by compass as you paddle your canoe across a large and foggy lake. The surest way to get lost is to try to aim straight at your destination on the other side of the lake and try to paddle directly to it through the dense fog, making no mistakes, drifting neither to the north or south, so that you will emerge from the fog exactly at your desired destination. Let's assume you actually reach the other side of the lake (this is not a guaranteed outcome, by the way). Let's assume that you didn't hit your destination exactly (an exceedingly safe assumption: if you hit your destination you should go home quick and buy a lottery ticket because such luck is rare and won't last). Let's assume that the shoreline looks like any wilderness shoreline: an even treeline of cedars and black spruce, low hills here and there, small bays, points, and inlets that look like the bays, points, and inlets all along almost any shore of almost any lake. And, let's assume that the fog is thick, so thick that you can only see about twenty feet in any direction. You've found the shore, but you have not found the desired landing. You can't see the landing from where you are floating, bobbing and fog-bound.

Do you go north or south to find the landing you were seeking? You don't know. How far do you go north before you decide you had better try going south? Without decent visibility and without clear geographical evidence, again you don't know. How long could you spend paddling north and then south and then maybe north again, hoping to blunder onto your destination? If the fog doesn't lift and you don't get lucky, we could be talking hours, and that's only if you haven't encountered other oddities that make your compass (and your luck) even worse. In a true wilderness under these circumstances, the chances of getting lost are better than the chances of getting found, which is a sobering realization.

So how do you avoid making the newspapers by becoming the objective of a massive search involving helicopters and bloodhounds? By making purposeful mistakes. Experienced wilderness travelers will aim, not for their exact destination, but for a point that is carefully (for example) south of their destination. They will try to make a mistake and will purposefully miss their destination so that when they finally reach the other side of the lake they will know that, wherever they are, exactly, they are south of the landing they wanted to reach. Because they have made a careful mistake, they know that if they go north they will hit the landing and continue on their way. It would still be possible to get lost, but you'd have to work a lot harder. Making mistakes is a good way to stay oriented, and to stay out of the newspapers.

So when we have finished with a Read-Around, whether we are working by ourselves or with a workshop group, we take time to make clear to everyone in the room that the next thing we will be doing is making mistakes. We know we will be making mistakes; we know pretty clearly which mistakes we will be making; and we know the ways the story we are exploring is usually read, which is often well to the north of where we are currently aiming to read it. Having established the customary context in which we are playing, we ask ourselves what we have heard, what we have noticed.

All sorts of things emerge from this investigation. People comment on particularly stylish or outrageous renderings of lines. People comment on our translation, finding places where it works, or doesn't. And people notice things about the text. Some lines are surprising all by themselves. Sometimes Jesus (for instance) says something, or does something, that simply seems odd. Sometimes there are lines that, while normal enough in themselves, fit together oddly, causing serious bumps in the road as we read. Sometimes these oddities and difficulties cause problems with the flow of the episode as we read. Everything seems to be moving in one direction, and suddenly there is an eddy, or even a complete reversal of flow. Such discoveries are interesting. Gospel texts, while not as long-used and polished as texts from Jewish Scripture, still have a long period of storytelling performance rubbed into them. Such an origin tends to rub off useless rough spots, and to intensify those oddities (in flow or fit) that are at the heart of the story.

So we listen carefully for such oddities. And when we find them, we set out to intensify them. This is where the fun (and the mis-taking) begins. If Jesus' words to the Syrophoenician woman (Mark, chapter 7) sound harsh, we make them harsher. If Jesus' refusal to acknowledge the presence of his mother and brothers (Matthew, chapter 12) is a little shocking, we play the scene as if his aggrieved mother were telling the story. If it is surprising that Jesus could fall asleep in the middle of a storm (Matthew, chapter 8), we let the experienced sailors tell the story.

And then we reverse the process. We play the harsh words to the Syrophoenician woman as if they were sweet and friendly. We let an apologist tell the story about his mother and brothers, and we look for ways to create other reactions to Jesus' little snooze aboard the boat. And then we play the scenes in another way. And another. And another. Each time we listen for what surprises us, what catches our ear, our eye, or our imagination.

As we play, making as many wild mistakes as possible, we often find ourselves drawn to odd little tensions within the texts we work with. The more ways we play the text, the more times we find ourselves caught by the same little tensions, no matter how we play the text. These tensions, these fractures, in the body of the text fascinate us, not because we delight in finding out how things don't work, but because we are devoted to discovering how it is that these texts *do* work, and what work they do. We are increasingly convinced that these tensions point us to the effort the texts we interpret make to make sense, a most difficult enterprise, indeed. Sometimes these tensions show (we think) the strain that is required as part of the effort to nail recalcitrant pieces into a coherent whole. Sometimes these tensions show (we think) that the original storyteller or her community did not fully agree with the sense that was being made. Sometimes (we think) these tensions point out central problems that Christians in the early generations of the Christian movement were working to solve. And sometimes we think that these tensions were woven into the text so as to create productive problems for future generations of tellers, hearers, and readers.

These last two moments are most important to us in our work. If we do, indeed, occasionally discover evidence of the strenuous work done by early Christian communities to make sense of difficult problems, sometimes this might point us to a fuller understanding of the history of the Christian faith and of the texts that feed that faith. And if we discover that the texts we interpret are constructed so as to provoke certain questions and problems in their audiences, then we may well have discovered something significant about the theological engine that drives the Christian faith, and about how that faith might continue to engage public imaginations.

This last possibility is most important. If these texts are built so as to provoke tense questions, then we have found something that we can play as storytellers and actors. You can't have a play (or an interesting story) without clash, without something that hooks the audience and gives them a reason to try to puzzle their way through the performance. If we occasionally discover one of these constitutive provocations, we will have discovered a way of weaving the gospels back into public imagining, public life and conversation.

Tensions in the Text, Tensions in the Context(s)

When we think we have found interesting tensions within a text, tensions that might even be constitutive of the text itself, we are then ready to begin making really interesting mistakes. The process to this point has been scattered, and a little random. We have picked through the text as hunter-gatherers, finding things wherever and whenever we found them. Now we tighten the focus of our work.

At this point in our work, we seek to understand these tensions we have found. Part of this understanding involves the historical and theological substance of the text and the tension. All the texts we work with have been read intensely for the better part of two millennia, some of them for considerably longer than that. Knowing the history of this intense reading and interpreting is crucial to sharpening our knowledge of the text we are working on. Sometimes this history confirms our sense of the tension by providing similar readings of the text, or by providing an interpretive context in which this new tension might be understood. When Victor of Antioch[2] (so long ago) notes the disruptive nature of the best-attested ending of Mark, or when Nils Dahl[3] (much more recently) notes the oddity caused when the title "Christ" is applied to Jesus (by being written on a sign and nailed to his cross) who seems not to warrant such a title, our own discoveries of tensions around these scenes suddenly have company. Company is good, if only because it helps us sharpen our sense of the significance of the tensions we have discovered.

This leads to another part of the process, a part that is most productive and also, perhaps, the hardest to explain and understand. When we discover tensions within the text, we try to assign those tensions to players in our troupe. If the tension is between characters, we assign a player to each character in an effort to clarify how the tension is formed and resolved (if it is resolved). If the tension (as also often happens) is between the lines even of a single character, then we likewise assign a player to each side of the tension in an attempt to clarify and understand how the tension works. Thus we might, to pick up on the tensions mentioned previously, assign one player to tell the end of Mark's story as if 16:8 is the final and proper ending to the story while assigning another player (or two or three) to react to the incompleteness of the end and provide (sequentially, perhaps) the extra padding that they feel is needed. Or we might give one player those lines that celebrate Jesus as the messiah, while another player would be given those lines (even if they were spoken by Jesus himself) that make him seem like the most unlikely candidate possible for such a title. And then we let the players clash with each other. Over and over. In various improvised settings. And we watch the clash, looking and listening for clues that will help us to understand the tensions that make the text what it is.

One of the most productive ways to clarify and understand the tensions within a text is to project them on the screen of tensions that we all know something about already, the screen of the tensions of everyday life. This part of this operation takes a little while to figure out. An example might help.

One of the scenes that we find most intriguing in Mark's story is the episode in which Jesus stills the storm (Mk. 4:35–41). The power and control he shows are incredible. The disciples' reactions are overwhelming. The diagnostic signs of faith are beyond human ability to produce, probably a main point in Mark's story. In the middle of this fascinating scene, Jesus is asleep in the boat in the midst of a terrifying storm. The disciples, some of whom made their living on the water, according to the story, know that they are dying. Jesus, who in this scene is in a boat for the first time, as reported in Mark's story, is sleeping. The tension found in the moment when the experienced sailors confront the sleeping landlubber is interesting. Interpreters have talked about the disciples' lack of faith, their lack of comprehension, and their needless fearfulness, so the standard way to play this scene would involve playing the disciples as cowards who will discover that they were wrong to be afraid. When we were working with this story (and aiming to make mistakes), we wondered how the tension between Jesus and the disciples would play if we granted that the disciples knew what was going on, that they, given their experience, knew when it was a good time to be afraid.

So we looked for a situation in regular life that would involve a character who was not afraid when she should have been. After many experiments with different backstories, a pair of our players performed the scene as if it were about a parent who was worried about her child's friends and her behavior. The child (mostly speaking Jesus' lines) was unconcerned, convinced that she was indestructible. The parent (mostly speaking the disciples' lines) was concerned, properly so, that her child did not show the ability to recognize dangerous situations. As we played the scene experimentally, we shifted the lines and fragments of lines back and forth between the characters to clarify the tension as much as possible, breaking the scene between our experimental characters in any way that helped us in our exploration. In the current final version (these things always change through time) the lines are divided as follows:

Mother

On that day when it was evening, he says to them:
    Let's go across to the other side.
So they leave the crowd and take him,

Daughter

    since he was already in the boat.
        Other boats were with him.

Mother

    A great windstorm arises;
        the waves beat into the boat,
        the boat is being swamped.

Daughter

        He was in the stern,

Mother

            his head on the pillow,
                sound asleep.
    They wake him up and say to him:
        Teacher, does it not matter to you that we are dying?

Daughter

> He woke up;
> he rebuked the wind
> and he said to the sea:

Mother

> Silence. Be still.

Daughter

> The wind stopped. There was a dead calm.
> He said to them:
> > Why are you afraid like this?
> > How do you not have faith?

Mother

And they feared a great fear,
> and they were saying to each other:

There is only a pair of sentences left in the story, but before we finish the scene, notice what we have so far. The scene develops normally. The mother attempts to maintain connection to her daughter, despite the daughter's insolence. The daughter attempts to make her point, to assert her adulthood and her ability to judge.

Then comes the final pair of sentences. Who should speak these words? The mother? The daughter? Both? Someone else, perhaps a father who had been silent up to this point? This was difficult to figure out. We tried everything we could think of. We moved the fragments back and forth between mother and daughter, looking for the mistake that would orient us. Then one time the mother took the first half of the last line, and the daughter took the last.

Mother

> Who is this guy?

Daughter

> Even the wind and the sea obey him.

Suddenly the scene was about the daughter's association with a man who might well, at least from the mother's point of view, be dangerous. The daughter, however, saw only his power, his attraction.

It may need to be said again: we are making mistakes here. This is nothing like what this scene is about. There is no mother and no daughter in the scene. There are no women reported at all. And there is no parent-child relationship to be found either. These elements of experimental play are there simply to clarify the tensions we find within the language of the text. But this way of playing this scene shines a powerful light on a major tension within Mark's larger narrative world, the tension between a character who departs from tradition and family, who even seems to go out of his way to offend them, and the family who had nurtured him, and (as the story develops) continue to attempt to nurture and claim him. This way of playing the scene raises the possibility that within Mark's story is a painful reflection on the wisdom of the development of the Christian movement away from Torah observance toward a communal life in which, as Paul wrote, Torah (and all the supportive structures that implied) had come to an end.

This is a reflection worth contemplating when interpreting the stilling of the storm. But we would never have bumped into this reflection without setting out to make mistakes.

What do we do with mistakes, once we have made them? We save them, we cherish them, and we throw them out, but only out to the compost heap, hoping for future fertility. Not everything works. Not everything contributes to the performances of the story that we have attempted so far. But everything is cycled back into the process out of which future performances and future interpretations will be created. Sometimes truly outrageous mistakes have to ripen, even to decay, for a while. And sometimes these truly outrageous mistakes end up demonstrating how well the old, comfortable reading of the text actually works.

When this happens, we find ourselves appreciating (from a new angle) the story of the healing of a blind man in Bethsaida (Mk. 8:22–26). Even if you don't immediately remember which story that is, because you know that a blind man is healed you already know that at the end of the scene sight triumphs over blindness. That's what we all know a healing story is supposed to do: those things that limit creation, hamper it, are to be removed. If you know the story, however, you know that it is not such a simple matter to get to the comfortable end of this story. In the middle, the audience is taken on a rather surprising detour.

Jesus attempts to heal the man (it has always worked before), and the man looks and sees trees walking. Not the outcome Jesus had anticipated, though the man might have settled for it, depending on how long he had been blind.

Jesus tries again. The result is more what audiences will have expected from Jesus, and just in the nick of time, because Jesus is headed toward Caesarea Philippi and the first prediction of his crucifixion. Anyone familiar with the history of the interpretation of these two scenes will, perhaps, remember that the detour, the surprise, the mistake (if you will) on the way to the healing has proved a useful thing for interpreters. Now they can use the healing story as a template for reading the story of Peter's confession of Jesus as the messiah. Now they can see that confession, too, as involving a detour, a surprise, and perhaps a mistake, one that earns Peter a rebuke from Jesus.

For our purposes, we simply hope to make such useful mistakes at least once in a while. And sometimes we do.

PART TWO: HOW TO MAKE MISTAKES

Pick a Story

Here's another set of suggested stories to explore. As always, there are many other stories that you could choose. These have the advantage of provoking the making of useful mistakes:

Trees Walking (Mk. 8:22–26);

And Throw It to the Dogs (Mk. 7:24–30)—only this time reverse the genders (see the following);

Who Is My Mother? (Matt. 12:46–50)—try this also with the genders reversed.

Warm Up

There are, of course, no magic warm-up exercises, no certain set of activities that will automatically guarantee the specific success of this session. The suggestions that I make are designed to help with the work you are attempting at this point in your exploration of this way of interpreting the Bible, but it should be noted that the success of this way of working does not hang on the notion that these exercises are so self-evidently brilliant that nothing could ever take their place. In fact, you might look at them and, more than once in a while, notice how utterly ordinary they are. You might decide that there is nothing too special about the exercises I suggest. You would be right.

Let me say it again: there are no magic warm-up exercises, or if there are such exercises, these are not them. Do not, on those grounds, decide to omit the warm-up. There is, indeed, a certain magic to the simple matter of physically preparing to interpret biblical texts. That physical preparation, strange as it is, is what makes this way of working quite different from any way you have worked before. It ought to be noted that the difference and advantage of working this way take a little time to become evident. You may well not have seen earth-shaking changes up to this point. It may all have seemed a little awkward and embarrassing. As Radar O'Reilly used to say on *M*A*S*H* when he could hear the helicopters coming before anyone else: "Wait for it."

Trust the process. Warm up.

Your warm-up needs to proceed from simple activities to more complex activities. The first things you do should be the sorts of transitional exercises that allow people to move from where they were before to where they are now. You will be able to track this progression by listening to the conversation that accompanies the beginning of the warm-up. It will mostly involve what people were doing before they began the session. This is good. You don't want the session to stay lodged in what was happening before, but trust the group to make its own transition. And pay attention to those topics of conversation that do not seem to go away. Sometimes those topics are matters that ought to be talked about before the group begins its work. Sometimes those topics contain the keys to what the group will be doing with biblical texts during the present session. Pay attention.

You could use the exercises that you used in the previous sessions. Here are some other exercises you can add to the process:

Space Substance

This is an exercise I first learned many, many years ago when I was part of a theater group that was using Viola Spolin's *Improvisation for the Theater* as a guide to learn improvisatory technique. The exercise still feels silly and wonderful after all these years. Spolin's book is still in print (after these many years), and you might very well want to find it and read her detailed description of this exercise.[4] Her suggestions for side-coaching are especially useful. You will recognize in Spolin the roots of many things that are central to this mode of biblical interpretation.

Read Spolin for the detail. Here's the nuts-and-bolts version.

Ask the people in your group to move freely around the space in which you are working, circulating, weaving in and out. Ask them to feel the space as they move through it. To help them feel the space, tell them that they are now moving through water. Ask them to feel the way the water supports and resists them as they move. Ask them to feel the water as it pushes against their legs, their arms, their whole body.

When they have explored the water thoroughly, tell them that the water has changed to pudding. Take them through the same set of physical explorations of this new space substance. Change the substance periodically, include helium, champagne, fire, molasses, and anything else you can think of.

Some of what you will see will look like the beginnings of dance (for good or for ill). Some will look like awkward and aimless milling about. Both are useful, and both are a good beginning. Draw attention always to the physicality of the movement, the totality of bodily involvement in the substance.

You might want to divide your group and create half of the group as an audience for the other half as they explore the substance. Remember to remind them of the crucial supportive role played by the audience. In this exercise the audience is an ally in the exploration of the substance, in the solving of the physical problem posed by your directions. When both halves of the group have served as audience, ask the group what they saw and noticed. Look and listen for those moments that revealed something of total physical involvement.

Musical Substance

When your group has explored these imaginary substances sufficiently, you might want to add the next level of complexity and support to the exercise. This variation is the same exercise, but done this time with music as the creator of the substance through which people will move.

Ask the people in your group to distribute themselves around the space in which you are working. Tell them that they will be moving through space just as they did in the previous exercise. Tell them to allow the music to create the nature of their physical involvement with the space as they move. Tell them to move, to listen, and not to think. You are not after planned or scripted choreography. You are not looking for cleverness. You are looking for physical involvement with the space that is shaped by the flow and development of the music. Tell them that as they move and explore they will encounter each other in the space. Direct them to let the music tell them what to do when they meet. Allow them some time to relax and focus, and begin playing the music.

Play any sort of music that seems interesting to you. In my experience it works best if the music does not have words attached. Words are turned into script (even when the language used is not spoken by any member of the group, oddly enough), and scripting short-circuits the process. Pick something that has changes and contrasts, something that will pose strong challenges to the people in your group. Initially it works best if you pick music that is quite abstract, perhaps even minimalist. You might want to investigate, for instance, the work of Aphex Twin, which is assembled electronic music, layered and odd. The shifts in tone and eruptions of sound draw useful exploration out of a group. As your group develops facility in this exercise, you might want to consider Stravinsky's "Rite of Spring." This music will provide an abstract program that will draw out all sorts of dramatic interaction from the group. Experiment and explore.

Columbian Hypnosis

Initial attempts at the preceding exercises are likely to yield a few moments of delightful physicality and longer stretches of self-conscious awkwardness. This is to be expected, especially if the people in your group thought they were going to be interpreting biblical stories when they joined up. Interpreting biblical stories involves sitting and thinking and talking, at least as it is usually practiced. The way of working with texts presented in this book is not usual, as you will have guessed.

This exercise helps people get around their self-consciousness.

Pair up the members of your group. If there is an odd number of people, make yourself a member of a pair as well. Ask each pair to select a guide and a follower. Tell the guide to hold up her hand before the face of the follower, about eight inches away with the palm out. Tell the follower that her whole task in life is to keep her face in exactly that relationship to the guide's hand. If the guide tilts her hand to the left, the follower tilts her head in response. If the guide pulls her hand back, the follower moves her head to follow the hand. If the guide moves her hand down to the floor, or around in a circle, or back and forth, or high into the air, or up and down all around the perimeter of the room, the follower's whole task is to keep her face eight inches away from the guide's hand, no matter where it goes. Tell them that the roles will be reversed after a while, so it might be a good idea for the first guides to be somewhat merciful.

When the people in your group have understood the directions, begin the exercise. Let them explore the problem posed by this exercise. If you do not have a partner, watch to see how people are engaging the problem. Look for those moments when people are working creatively and with focus. You will see many such moments, and you will see people who are normally physically restrained now performing all manner of contortions as they focus intensely on their objective.

After a sufficient time of exploration, direct the people to switch roles. Watch to see how this is accomplished. Remember that this shift returns everyone to the very beginning. It is a very different thing to be a follower than to be a guide, and this difference will yield a certain awkwardness that will become part of the problem that is to be solved by the people in your group.

It is frequently useful to do this exercise also with an audience. If the group is thoroughly physically involved, you might want to split the group in halves: half audience, half performers. If self-consciousness is still a problem for the group, you might want, instead, to pick a single pair to perform. This works best if you pick a guide who is physically graceful and inventive (if you have a dancer in the group, pick her), and if you pick a follower who is good-hearted but self-conscious. This pairing will show the group something that will surprise them. Do not tell anyone why you have picked them. This is important.

Give this performing pair the initial directions all over again. Emphasize that the follower has a single purpose in life: to maintain her current physical relationship to the guide's hand. Remind the pair that you will switch their roles later, and emphasize the importance of mercy. Remind the audience that their role is to help the players achieve their objective. Direct them to begin.

When the players have finished the exercise, ask the audience what they noticed. Help them to see the moments when self-consciousness vanished. It is likely that there will have been many such moments.

Notice particularly the moments when the first follower moved with a physical grace that was surprising. These moments happen because of the intense physical focus that is at the heart of this exercise. Point out that the scenes you will be playing involve the same kind of physical following and guiding, the same kind of focused interaction, though less abstract. As you work on the scenes you will be exploring, look for moments in which this is true. There will be a few. Not many, but a delightful few. Build on them.

By the way, I have no idea why this exercise is called "Columbian" hypnosis. That's just what it was called the first time I learned it from one of my students.

Do a Read-Around and a Gesture-Around

As noted, this is a permanent feature. This is especially true when you are working with a story that everyone already knows too well. Build on what you began last session. Expect this exercise to begin to bear a little fruit. Expect also that better things are coming. Always spend time at the end gathering what the group has seen, heard, and noticed.

Stage a Tug-of-War

This also is worth doing again, especially since you are after (eventually) a backstory (remember the scene with the mother and daughter that was used to crack open the "stilling of the storm" scene in the first part of this chapter?) that will match the tensions you have found. Use the tug of war to explore the tensions within the text in finely grained detail. If you can get clear about the shape of the tension in the text, you will have a much easier time finding a backstory that reproduces the tensions helpfully. For this time through the exercise, shift players ("tuggers") frequently to increase the odds that your group will find something illuminating about the tensions of the text. Pay careful attention to what you see and hear, and encourage the audience to do so as well. Someone may have the hammer that cracks the text open.

Attempt Some First Embodiments

This goes hand-in-hand with the tug-of-war exercise. In actual practice you will likely attempt an embodiment, elaborate a tentative backstory, play it as a tug-of-war, and move back to attempting another embodiment. Sometimes the process will just spin from attempt to attempt, making no noticeable progress. Sometimes the process will seem more like a purposeful spiral, burrowing into the story you are exploring. Trust the process either way. I'm not always sure, at the time, which is which.

Use the process to develop facility with elaborating the backstory. Think up more and more inventive ways to link the tensions of the text to tensions that people know something about. Encourage wild inventiveness. Do not worry if some of the resulting scenes seem too risky ever to play in front of an audience. When that starts happening, it is a sign that your group is starting to succeed, that people are starting to trust the text to take care of itself. This is crucial. Even more important, they are starting to trust each other. If they trust the text and each other, they can do almost anything. Now the real fun begins.

Necessary Multiplicity

Even after you identify the tensions in the text and even after you start playing the scenes experimentally, there will still be occasions when your players will slip back into standard-issue normalcy. That is not necessarily a problem. Some things are best when they are normal. But normalcy is overrated, if only because of the way human beings use the notion of what is "normal." There is hidden in the word the notion of a norm, a measuring stick, a template, a cookie cutter. That means that human beings use the notion of what is "normal" to avoid encountering surprises. Without surprises there is no truth. Or at least the truth you find is the least interesting sort.

So, if the scenes are becoming formulaic, you might want to try creating some new problems for your players. For instance:

Hidden Objectives

If you have tried several different ways of working with a story, you will have developed a sense of how the tensions are set. Take the players in the scene aside and give them instructions. Give to each an objective they *must* reach, no matter what. Pick the objectives so that they conflict with each other and so that they line up with the tensions in the text. Turn the players loose and let them try to solve the problem you have set for them.

As you watch their attempts to play the scene, look for those moments when each player is holding tight to her objective. There will be such moments. Notice them and remember them. There will also be the other moments, times when players abandon their objectives and start avoiding the clash the scene requires. At such moments, remind them (even in the middle of the scene) to stick with their objectives. It matters that they work to reach their goals, *no matter what*. Such determination will make the tensions in the text pop out into the open. Surprises are to be expected.

As with all other exercises, finish this exercise by gathering what members of the group have seen, heard, and noticed. They will surely have seen things that you did not. They will surely have noticed things that the players in the scene were not aware of. Follow those leads. Listen for the surprises, for new insights about how the text is, and is not, working. Listen especially for those moments when the structure of the tension seems wrong, when (for instance) you run across something "Jesus would never say." Those are sometimes the very best moments. It is, of course, possible (even likely) that the players have simply made a mistake, one that leads nowhere. Good. It is also possible, however, that the mistake you have just made is one that will open up the text, either because you will now have to find ways to push against the mistake you just made, or because you will discover that the "mistake" you made was not so mistaken after all. Maybe Jesus sometimes *does* say things he would never say.

Gender Bending

One especially productive mistake you can make any old time involves switching genders. You will have noticed by now that a great many of the characters in biblical stories are male. With the assumed baritone voice come many unspoken assumptions about this large crowd of characters. These assumptions will frequently deform interpretation and seal it so you don't even notice the deformation. Sometimes all it takes to crack open a story is a simple switching of gender roles. If the scene has two men talking, play it with two women talking. The women are not to attempt to pretend to be men (though this can be interesting when it reveals cross-gender assumptions about gender). Instead, they are to play the scene as if it were written for women. Likewise it can be fascinating to play those scenes in which Jesus (for instance) interacts with a woman with the genders crossed. Some of the most interesting oddities in the stories will pop into view if you do this.

In all of this, remember that the whole aim of this session is to make mistakes. It would be nice if the mistakes turned out to be productive ones, but that's not a requirement. You are only trying to learn how to make interesting mistakes. There are some *very* interesting mistakes you can make with gender.

Some Final Words about Mistakes and Multiplicity

There are some final matters that need attention at this point. You have gathered a group of explorers. You have begun to physically explore biblical texts. You have begun to learn to be silly and serious together. And, most difficult of all, you have begun practicing how to make multiple mistakes together. Here are some things to think about as you work through this process.

Honoring Your Group

Multiplicity means many things, not surprisingly, perhaps. One important thing it means is that you have more than one person in your gathered group. That means that you have more than one perspective in your gathered group. That means that you have disagreements within your group. And that means that at some points you (if you are functioning as the leader of the group) will need to practice honoring the group when it disagrees with you. Sometimes this is pretty easy. Sometimes it will be immediately clear that the group has come up with an idea that is clearly new, delightfully fascinating, and far superior to any idea you (the leader!) had ahead of time. But sometimes the group (as a whole or in part) will want to go somewhere you (the leader, after all!) would never, ever want to go.

This is where this way of working with texts begins to be uniquely valuable. And also painful. Sometimes you will go home from a work-session and complain that the group won't let you do what you want.

This is exactly what should happen. Practice honoring the leads the group wants to follow, not because you are always wrong, but because they might have found a way to work together to be even more right. Or you could practice honoring their leads as an exercise in making productive mistakes. Any way you do it, *do it.* You will encounter surprises and provocations. That was, if you remember, one of the goals you had when you started on this adventure.

Honoring Your Outsiders

This is where the diversity of the group you have gathered begins to pay off. If you have a group of insiders and only insiders, the text will still surprise you, and you will be drawn into fascinating mistakes. And your work will be wonderfully productive. These texts are just like that.

But if you have gathered a group that also includes creative and courageous outsiders, you will have a chance to make some truly interesting mistakes. Outsiders have the advantage of not knowing how the story is *supposed* to go. They are more likely to come up with readings that are simply atypical, surprising, and sometimes simply mistaken. This is the point at which the business of provoking the gospel imposes ethical demands. If you are aiming to make truly useful mistakes, you will need to remember to carefully honor the mistakes made by your outsiders. The tendency is for the insiders to correct the outsiders, to tell them "what everyone knows." While such scolding is probably well-intended, it is destructive to the process you have been working to establish. If you are aiming to learn to provoke the gospel, to call it out of the text, out of the group, and out of the audience, you will need, as a group, to practice honoring outsiders, especially when they make new kinds of mistakes. New mistakes are gifts from God.

Homework

There is always homework. It's still a good idea to go to the theater. It's still a good idea to go to the movies. You might want to look for the television listings for the show "Inside the Actors Studio," which is on the cable network Bravo. Week after week actors and directors are interviewed. Sometimes the interviews are no more than mildly interesting. But every once in a while an actor cracks open something about the way she works and you will suddenly understand what you have been attempting to do in these worksessions.

You will also benefit from continuing to watch for the pull-push of regular life. At work, at the store, anywhere you are, look for the ways people pull and push as they talk and negotiate their regular activities.

Imagine the tug-of-war that is being staged. What leads to victory in these contests?

Imagine the effect of restaging any of these contests with the genders switched. Which contests would change? Which would not change? Which "tugs" only work if they are done by males? Which only work for females?

In all of this, watch for the physical contest, the physical reality of the interaction. Watch the hands, watch the feet, watch the knees, watch the whole bodies.

Suggested Reading

Amit, Yairah. *Reading Biblical Narratives: Literary Criticism and the Hebrew Bible*. Minneapolis: Fortress, 2001.

Berman, Art. *From the New Criticism to Deconstruction: The Reception of Structuralism and Post-Structuralism*. Urbana: University of Illinois, 1988.

Spolin, Viola. *Improvisation for the Theater*. Evanston, Ill.: Northwestern University Press, 1963.

Lecoq, Jacques. *The Moving Body: Teaching Creative Theatre*. New York: Routledge, 2001; first published in French as *Le corps poetique*, Actes Sud-Papiers, 1997.

4

Holding Together / Coming Apart

I tell my story the way I remember, the way I want. . . .
I have to tell this story every day, add to it, revise, invent the parts
I forget or never knew. . . . No one but me carries it all
and no one will, unless . . .

—Michael Dorris, *A Yellow Raft in Blue Water*

The following pages are dedicated to my children and
grandchildren. My children, especially, are responsible for my efforts
here. They often suggested that a written report of this nature would be
desirable and that—when time permitted—I should jot down some
of the things that I remember about this period in my life. For
[my children] the years remembered here certainly had some influences
in my life that—to some extent—were the bases for my actions and
reactions to them as the years moved on. Everything that happens to
us—be it big or small, catastrophic or pleasant, seemingly important
or of no consequence—does something to our pattern of thinking
and reaction that influences our lives forever. These years certainly
had an indelible effect on me and some of this was bound
to rub off on them in varying degrees.

—Heimer W. Swanson, Rigger, Service Company,
508th Parachute Infantry Regiment, 82nd Airborne Division,
Twists, Tangles, and Turns

PART ONE:

WHY TO DISCOVER HOW STORIES HOLD TOGETHER AND COME APART

If remembering is the task any human community asks of its members, I find myself in some trouble. I could never hold my father's stories together. The fault was mine, not his.

My father was an essential farm worker. His exemption from military service identified him as such. He could have contributed to the war effort by working with his father, plowing the heavy soil of the Red River Valley in northern Minnesota with a horse-drawn plow, planting and harvesting grain that would be processed into food and fiber for the nation and its soldiers. He could have, but he did not.

He turned in his exemption. He left home and began a journey that took him from coast to coast in the United States and across the Atlantic Ocean to England, France, and Germany. All this though he had never before been more than thirty-five miles from the place he was born.

My father had wanted to be a pilot, but when he enlisted, they didn't need any pilots. He became instead a paratrooper, a member of the 82nd Airborne. At least that way he got to be in an airplane for the take-off. So he said.

My father told few stories about those days, and he told those few in scraps and scattered bits. Perhaps it was that he had not been in combat, and he did not presume to tell stories for those who could not tell them. Perhaps it was that we children were too intensely interested in our own stories ever to ask properly. Perhaps he told us more stories than I remember, but, being inattentive, I never managed to hold his stories together well enough to remember them. In any case, after his retirement he consented to write for us, his children and grandchildren, an account of those days. A report.

As he says, he "jotted it down." He provided a written, printed artifact that we can hold, and read, and consult. A book. But it is more than merely a book, which could simply be a list of dates and details, a box of ragged remembrances; it is a story. It has, and provides for us, what we had always lacked (probably through inattention): a plot, a wholeness, a beginning, a middle, and an end. And because it has those basic features of a story, it is now something we can remember, and think about. Now it holds together. In this chapter I explore the matter of how stories hold together, especially of how gospel stories hold together. And, since what is at stake in studying and telling gospel stories is the matter of re-membering Jesus, I will explore what difference it would make for the stories to hold together, and what difference it would make if they did not.

Making Sense by Holding Together

Aristotle, of course, long ago had already understood my father and the effect of his "jotting down" of his stories. A proper drama (and by extension, a proper story), said Aristotle, is one that has a beginning, a middle, and an end.

> A beginning is that which is not itself necessarily after anything else, and which has naturally something else after it; an end is that which is naturally after something itself, either as its necessary or usual consequent, and with nothing else after it . . .[1]

And in between comes the middle, tense with surprises, reversals, discoveries, and action. Aristotle's prescription is simple and powerful. Art is distinguished from raw nature, he says, by virtue of having a beginning, a middle, and an end. Matter is eternal, and so is nature, so is life, but art must start and stop. It must begin somewhere purposeful and stop somewhere satisfying. And in between the beginning and end is the coherent middle. The middle holds together because one scene leads to another. The middle holds together because each scene, each theme, each narrative arc echoes those that went before, and because each will set up its own echoes in the story to come. In the secured space between beginning and end, words bind themselves together into skeins of sentences because of the generative power of their sounds and significations. Sentences knit themselves into paragraphs because their rhythms suggest new rhythms, new silences. And paragraphs contrive to join with paragraphs in a dance that swirls, bumps, crashes, and weaves itself through whole actions having magnitude, worthy of thought.[2] All this between the artifice of a beginning and an end.

These stories cannot be random; we will not have them so. The words must tie themselves together; the paragraphs must dance. Above all, they must make sense. The manufacturing metaphor is important here. Aristotle knew long ago that we make sense artfully, as carefully as artists and artisans practice their crafts. Because what we are making is sense, it is incumbent upon us that we make it well. The stories we tell must make sense because we tell stories for the sake of order, to hold ourselves together in the roaring midst of raw randomness. As Frank Kermode argues, we tell stories to discover the meaning of things that baffle us, and if we can't discover the meaning, we invent it. We make sense.[3]

Annie Dillard has called this activity "doodling on the walls of the cave," and sees it to be the essential product of the human race.[4] Dillard's image of doodling seems, in one way, just right. Human beings are unstoppable storytellers. We do not have to put "Tell Stories Now" in our daily planners to be sure that we will tell them. Stories come out of us without our thought just like doodles come out of a pen.

But Dillard's image is also just wrong (in a beautifully intentional way). "Doodling" calls to mind the aimless and pointless clumsy decoration (or defacement) of the blank spaces around useful text in purposeful documents. "Doodling" is trivial, insubstantial. But out of our doodling come not just transient sketches but also elaborate narrative pictures, some of these pictures taking the form of very old stories that we continue to tell, old manufactured sense that endures even as the world changes and mutates, becomes industrial and postindustrial, technological and posttechnological. Dillard knows this.

These old stories that we continue to tell are amazingly durable. For example, European-American ethnologists have repeatedly written the obituary for the Native American tradition of oral story, but the rumors of its demise have been greatly exaggerated.[5] As Leslie Marmon Silko demonstrates in her book *Storyteller*, oral stories mutate and migrate, but they continue to shape the worlds of those who tell them, hear them, read them, and tell them again. The old stories support the maintenance of traditional languages, stable community forms, well-worn tools of wisdom that human communities pass along through time and change. But, as Silko makes clear, the old stories endure past even the loss of traditional language and traditional community life. Too much ethnological work of the past has imagined that traditional Native American oral story could only be preserved (note the embalming metaphor) as a romantically remembered relic of a past ideal world. As Silko notes, and as has been demonstrated over and over even in those Native American communities where traditional languages have been largely lost, the old stories have a power to shape worlds and shape lives.[6] This is some durable doodling.

Because we tell stories to figure out the delights or disasters that erupt new and out of nowhere, some of this doodling also takes the form of massive movements in popular culture. For instance, consider science fiction. In a world newly frightened by the technology of mass destruction, of bombs delivered silently from the other side of the world, rocketing out of the sky to shatter quiet, unsuspecting communities, science fiction movies in the 1950s told stories of dangerous, threatening aliens from space. Other eras told more hopeful stories about space and the beyond (notably the Tom Swift stories my father read as a child), but a world shocked by Hiroshima, Nagasaki, Dresden, and the London blitz needed to figure out human survival in the face of threats that dropped out of the sky. Times had changed, and the doodling changed, too.

Sometimes this new doodling takes the form of the fragmented and violent stories that abused children write for their grade school teachers, stories that take revenge while being careful never to name the crime that needs avenging. Faced with a father who attacks, a mother who destroys, a community that does not protect, such children fight back the only way they can, by writing frightening stories that blow the violence outward, inward, or both. All of this doodling, whatever its form, and however disturbing, all of this doodling is profoundly human. All of it is devoted to the central task of creating order and coherence, of making sense where otherwise there would be none. We insist on telling stories that hold together; if we did not, we would come apart.

And So We Tell Whole Stories

The storytellers I work with and talk with spend a great deal of time studying what holds a story together, what makes it a whole story. They hunt for the coherences that will let them remember the story and tell it: arcs and themes, tensions and resolutions, references and echoes, anything that will hold the story together, both for them and for the audiences who will hear it. Audiences ask for the same kind of coherence storytellers seek. They ask because they are human beings who must remember, who must wind their worlds in stories—if they are ever to understand them. They ask for coherence because they expect that their investment of time (they could, after all, have gone bowling instead) will yield (at least) some returned glimpse of sense, order, hope, or insight. And they ask for coherence for the same reasons storytellers ask: coherence is part of the artifice that makes the story rememberable and tellable. The question is: how do stories hold together? There are at least three possible answers.

Stories Hold Together Because of Contextuality

For a storyteller, the hunt for coherence begins with the atoms of the story, with the episodes, the scenes. In biblical texts it begins with the pericope, the piece that is "cut around," the preaching text that is cut out of the larger gospel story. It is perhaps ironic that, in order to discover what holds a story together, a storyteller takes it apart, disassembling it, dissecting it, taking it down to its smallest pieces, but that is where the hunt begins. Having found the smallest piece of the story that is still somehow whole, a storyteller looks for the ways this pericope, this episode, this scene touches the story around it. Each piece of a larger story comes after and before another piece. Each piece is part of something that might be a dance, a flow, a narrative arc. So a storyteller carefully touches these small bits of the story to the other small bits next to it, to see what sticks together. As noted in the last chapter, a storyteller working with Mark's story notices that Peter's confession of Jesus' identity (8:27ff) immediately follows the oddest healing story in all the gospels: Jesus heals a blind man but needs two tries to get it right. The second attempt, which brings the man up to acceptable visual acuity, is necessary because the first attempt leaves the man able only to see what look like trees walking. How odd. If you touch this scene to Peter's confession, you begin to wonder if Mark's story understands Peter's initial understanding of messiahship to be equally wooden, requiring amelioration, further explication. Maybe. Maybe not. But the immediate context sets a storyteller up to look for ways to play these stories next to each other.

A few chapters later, Jesus and his learners are returning to Jerusalem after a night in Bethany. They pass a fig tree. Jesus sees leaves. He looks for figs. He finds none, which is not surprising since it is not the season for figs. He curses the tree, calls for it to be fruitless, to cease to be part of God's fruitful and multiplying creation. This is odd. The apparent anger would, perhaps, be odd enough, especially in contemporary reading communities where careful social discipline has shaped people always to respond moderately. In such communities, Jesus, with his anger, breaks a first rule of community life: Don't get carried away. That would be bad enough, but it gets worse. It is not the season for figs. His anger is not just excessive, it is ill-timed and reveals either botanical ignorance or a propensity to make unreasonable demands. Either one is troublesome.

When a storyteller touches this scene to what follows, interesting trouble begins. In the next scene, Jesus gets carried away in the Temple. What is a storyteller to make of this? Interpreters concoct various justifications for Jesus' actions, mostly granting him some cover behind an imagined provocation, but a storyteller is stuck with the unreasonable anger of the preceding scene, with a context that complicates telling the Temple scene as a case of righteous anger. And then comes the next scene, where the fig tree is found to have withered to its root, which Jesus explains as a visual aid for faith(fulness). And what voice will make this attempt at justification work? Good question. Context causes such interesting problems, and these problems help hold the story together.

Stories Hold Together Because of Intratextuality

Stories hold together in another way as well. Surely episodes hold tight to the episodes that touch them and to those that link with them to form recognizable arcs through the telling. But episodes, even sentences and words, also hold together with other parts of a story. When this intratextual linking takes the form of obvious echo, old redaction critical studies provide helpful analyses of the phenomenon. When this linking relies on hook-words or on patterns of word use, the old word studies generated during the reign of biblical theology again prove useful. But the gospels (like any story) hold together also because episodes, sentences, and words stick to any part of the story, any episode, any sentence, any word, related or not. Every part of a story is sticky, and will stick even randomly to anything it touches.

That means that part of a storyteller's analysis will involve working agglomeratively, creating bulging masses of pieces of the gospel stuck together to see what happens. For instance, what happens in the gospel of Mark when you stick the death of John the Baptist onto the death of Jesus? These two episodes are obviously linked, part of the same narrative arc, but there are still surprises. Both John and Jesus die, executed by authorities almost on a whim. John is executed by Herod, pretender to the title "King of the Jews." John is beheaded. Jesus is executed by Pilate, crucified beneath a placard that identified him as the King of the Jews. After the execution, supporters collect the bodies in each case, but John's headless body is called a πτωμα (ptoma) while Jesus' crucified body is called a σωμα (soma). Both Greek words are properly translated as "corpse," but they play in slightly different fields of usage. Sticking these two episodes together requires the storyteller to decide how different these words are. Is John's corpse deader than Jesus' corpse? Sticking these two episodes together at least requires the storyteller to wonder if ancient Jewish usage reacted differently to a headless corpse than to a whole one, or if Mark is prefiguring the resurrection in his choice of words, or if Mark might be making a comment on the social and theological future of John's leaderless movement. Each possibility will yield a differently shaded telling of Mark's story.

Or a storyteller might stick the episode involving Jesus' death onto the scene in which he stills the storm on the lake. Taken separately, the two episodes have each been read by pulpits-ful of interpreters so as to provide edifying pictures of true faith and love. But when the two episodes are stuck together, made to dance with each other, suddenly things sound different. When the disciples find themselves in the midst of a deadly storm, they find Jesus asleep. "Don't you care that we're dying?" they ask. "How do you not have faith?" asks Jesus. But when Jesus finds himself caught, done to death on the cross, he echoes the disciples' cries of fear, not his own, too-calm words after he stills the storm. "My God, why?" he shrieks. Suddenly Jesus' ringing words of faith (spoken in a moment of enforced calm in the boat) rebuke not his disciples but himself. "How do you not have faith?" he asks. How indeed?

Some of these intratextual links reveal what might be narrative arcs. Some reveal nothing more than interesting quirks in Mark's story. And some can be taken as hints of themes and structures that might work to hold Mark's story together, both for teller and for audience.

Stories Hold Together Because of Intertextuality

Storytellers study stories, looking for arcs and themes, looking for anything that might be useful to hold the story together. Sometimes they find a coherent context, sometimes an embracing intratext. And sometimes what they find is that their story is held together by what deconstructive interpreters call an "intertext," a text external and even extraneous to the story being studied, a text that provides another way of reading and discovering the tensions and fractures that hold a text together.

The word "deconstruction" draws fire and wrath from some who interpret texts, and sometimes the reaction is justified. Some of what passes under that name seems no more than an adolescent infatuation with taking things to bits and then asserting that nothing works. No big surprise. If that is all that deconstruction offers, I would imagine that we could all do without it. But I hear something else in the word. Maybe it is because my grandfather was an old-fashioned, hammer-and-handsaw carpenter, but I hear a carpentry metaphor in the word "deconstruction," and this metaphor has always shaped my experience with deconstruction.

There are two ways old buildings are approached by people in the building trades. One involves sledgehammers, shattered plaster and lath, clouds of choking dust, and totally new construction to replace old, decayed work. And if the builders cannot patch and repair the old with new construction, they tear everything down; they make a hole in the ground where there used to be a building.

I remember an episode of the television show *This Old House*. On this show old houses are examined, diagnosed, and restored, week after week, now for more than twenty years. Week after week, foundations are examined, walls are opened up, problems are found. Week after week, master carpenter Norm Abrams says to contractor Tommy Silva, "Well, you never know what you'll find until you open the wall up." On one episode, the problems in the house started out bad and rapidly got worse. One room was in particularly bad shape. Everything the carpenters touched turned to dry rot and revelations of shoddy construction. At the end of the episode, after the shell-shocked homeowners had been told the bad news, after they had been escorted off screen to lick their (considerable) financial wounds, while the smiling host was closing down the episode for the week, the carpenters were heard (accidentally, I assume) in the background asking what they should do. "Get the SawzAll," said Tommy Silva, calling for the reciprocating saw, the tool of last resort. A SawzAll cuts through everything: wood, plaster, nails, pipes. It is not, shall we say, a tool much used by cabinetmakers, but then the carpenters were not, at this point, engaged in anything delicate like cabinetmaking. The wall was coming out. Everything would be razed. Nothing would be saved, because nothing *could* be saved. This is called, in the building trades, demolition. Nothing is worth saving, and nothing will be saved. The dumpster will be full. Get the SawzAll.

That is not the only way old houses are handled, however, not on this television show or anywhere else. There is another approach, slower, more painstaking, an approach that removes each stud, each joist, sometimes even each piece of lath carefully, using tools like a cat's paw and a nailpuller instead of sledge hammers and reciprocating saws. The approach intends to preserve the old work, discover its genius, repair what has been weakened over the years, and replace the original materials, replicating the original construction. This way of working is not called demolition. It is called deconstruction. Just so.

Demolition or deconstruction? SawzAll or cat's paw? The decision is based on determinations about the soundness of the building, about the genius of the original tradespeople who built it. The two approaches to old edifices yield different results and different techniques. The differences matter. It is indeed true that some of what gets called "deconstruction" in interpretation ought more properly to be called "demolition." At this point I share my grandfather's passion for precision. If what is going on is demolition, have the sense to call it that. But if the practice is genuine deconstruction, then call it deconstruction and use the proper tools. The differences do indeed matter.

And so a storyteller sometimes deconstructs a story, takes it to bits and then puts it back together. The aim is to discover how the story has worked, and has not worked, through all these years. The aim of such deconstructive work is to see into the story the way a good carpenter sees into a building, and, as Norm Abrams says, "You never know what you'll find until you open up the wall." Just so.

And so a storyteller experiments. All parts of a story are touched together, even wildly disparate parts, just to see what happens. Sometimes there is music. Sometimes things blow up.

This experimental process is not limited, however, just to the story itself. Some of the most productive work happens as a result of touching stories to each other, stories that have nothing at all to do with each other. This practice explores what is commonly called "intertextuality." Some of what poststructuralist interpreters examine under the heading of intertextuality are simple citations and quotations, conscious or otherwise. This work is useful, though it should be noted that pretty much anyone can recognize such explicit intertextual citations. Some intertextual work focuses on subtler forms of citations, patterns of influence, again conscious or not. And again, anyone who is a cultural insider can recognize the inside jokes that are a regular, and valuable, part of intertextual surveys.

Intertextual study becomes most interesting, however, at the point it recognizes that any set of texts, even texts that are wildly disparate, will dance together intertextually if given the chance. In such work, reading strategies rooted in one text will be applied to another text. Love stories will be read as war stories (and *vice versa*), with intriguing results (you might want to review the discussion about making mistakes in the previous chapter). Plot structures (which is to say, patterned expectations) native to one text as part of its own genre will be hunted for in other texts, no matter what genre they are judged to belong to, again with intriguing results. Notions of narrative tension and release, and the mechanisms appropriate to them, will be applied anywhere they might be useful. Storytellers who work intertextually discover that the story they are learning to tell sticks to other stories, even to stories that seem most definitely extraneous. Stories that have never met, never imagined each other, these stranger stories still stick together, still dance the same dance because, as the structuralists and their forerunners showed us, there is a relatively small set of possible narrative structures, a limited bag of tricks and tensions with which storytellers can play.[7] As a result, every part of every story sticks to every other story that winds itself through the same narrative structures.

All the stories that a culture tells itself stick together, bump into each other, and shape each other. This makes good cultural and anthropological sense. But only when I listened closely to a particularly conservative (and "culture-rejecting")[8] group of students on the campus where I teach did I see how thoroughly this is true. It happened during a course I teach on reading the gospels. These students, conservative Christians, were explaining the Atonement to the class, intending to counteract the results of the explorations that had been conducted by other members of the class. Those results of the explorations were insufficiently orthodox for this group of students, so they used their presentation time to make their own argument. They made a good and honorable argument for their own view of the meaning of Jesus' death. According to their construal of this central event for Christians, Jesus was engaged in a war with Satan. It was an all-out war, bloody and violent, and Jesus was finally ambushed and executed. The battle seemed to be over, but then came the resurrection, which changed everything. Jesus, being raised from the dead, now took the battle into the stronghold of the enemy. His victory was final and total, and he rode off alone, his work completed.

The members of the class listened closely. Some agreed with the sketch presented. Some disliked the violence it embodied. Some found it exciting, in a cinematic sort of way. And then one member of the class noted that what they had sketched was (roughly) the plot of the Arnold Schwarzenegger movie, *Conan the Barbarian*. And they were right. Conan is even crucified.

So who stole the story from whom? The answer to that question is, "Yes." Everybody stole it from everybody. Images and plots and expectations and complications and resolutions all dance together in a culture, trading stories and phone numbers. Over time, everyone gets acquainted with everyone else.

The writers of *Conan the Barbarian* borrowed pieces of a long line of conflict and release stories, among them cultural readings of Jesus' career. My students, as contemporary readers of the gospels, looked with eyes accustomed to the conventions of American adventure movies. Thoroughly secular Americans talk about "redemption" in a way that is clearly borrowed from the language and narrative of Americans who reject American culture in favor of something more "spiritual." Love stories, war stories, gospels, and adventure stories—all stories ride together on public transportation. And everybody makes friends with everybody, eventually.

Objections to Intertextuality, or "Slippery Scripture"

Not every reader of biblical narrative will agree with the argument just advanced. Even in the face of the apparent interweaving of gospel and adventure movie, many readers will argue that such an approach to biblical texts goes wrong from the beginning. Many readers will argue that Mark's status as Inspired Scripture lend it a certain slipperiness that lets it slide, unsullied, through crude secularity. Others will argue that secular stories stick to Inspired Scripture, drawing their true reading from it, while Inspired Scripture itself sticks to nothing.

Biblical storytellers must take these arguments seriously. While it is easy to caricature the viewpoint that Inspired Scripture is made slippery by its divine status (the caricature shows even in the Use of Capital Letters), responsible interpreters need to step back from caricature and listen to the aims and implications of the possible views here.

With the expectation that Inspired Scripture is somehow slippery, that it provides its own determinative interpretive context, comes the expectation that human *being* (even in its stories) is not simply self-caused and self-absorbed. This is a notion with important implications. With this notion of slippery Scripture comes the expectation of an address from outside, from beyond (which is to say, somehow, from God), or of an address from within, moving outward (which is to say, from the community to an external world). While there surely are people who have not reflected on the difficulties involved in speaking of an "outside" to the universe (the very word "universe" implies that everything is encompassed *within* it), while there surely are naïve individuals who have never wondered at the way a disconnected heavenly realm becomes superfluous to human existence and experience in a universe experienced as a creation of God, still the main proponents of linguistic separation are neither naïve or lacking in reflective power. George Lindbeck, for instance, is no stranger to the difficulties involved in imagining an address to the world from outside the world. But still he maintains that the essential character of the texts and traditions of the Christian movement, all of its use of language, is revealed only when it is understood as being an address from God to a beloved creation. For all of the lines and patterns of intertextual influence that can be discerned and demonstrated, still biblical narrative functions, and is properly understood, as an alien word embodied in human words and forms.[9]

From this basic understanding some Christians (not Lindbeck) will conclude that revelation slides into the world in biblical narrative, picking up nothing on its way in. Interpretation consists in sliding revelation out into the broader world, where it will attract everything and be affected by nothing. In this view, any interpretive connection flows from the biblical text to an (almost) extraneous world, and never the other way. As I was told at a conference I attended, "There are faithful interpretations and unfaithful interpretations. Similarities between features in biblical narratives and features in other cultural narratives are nothing more than shallow resemblances. They are not even interesting to a faithful interpreter." Again, it is easy to caricature such a position, but it is important to honor the insistence on God's speaking voice, addressing God's creation. And, to cite a voice of considerably greater sophistication, it is important to note that George Steiner argues that any narrative asserts a transcendent anchor, a rootage not just (but also) in a real world, a rootage sunk deep in a governing notion of God, who guarantees real coherence and correspondence.[10] This argument deserves careful attention.

So we grant it that some kind of externality provides something like stability, some kind of guarantee. If Scripture somehow comes from outside of transient human community, then it has a kind of solidity, a kind of reliability, that seems useful.

But what is the status of that stability, that externality? It is here that fights over deconstruction (and poststructuralism, and postmodernism in general) typically get serious. Each side comes to the field armed with more or less accurate caricatures of the other side. Most of the caricatures are mostly accurate because there is plenty of antic foolishness to be observed all around this issue. I will forego the usual game of thrust and parody, not because it's not fun, but because the matter at hand is too serious for such diversions. We are considering what it is that holds stories together, what it is that makes them memorable and effective, what it is that makes them productive in the sense noted by Annie Dillard.[11]

It is first to be noted that, while there is an overabundance of adolescent practitioners of deconstructive interpretation who delight in demonstrating (with an admirably stable diligence) that nothing can possibly hold together, deconstruction as explored by Jacques Derrida is not an exercise in adolescent nihilism. In fact, as he notes in his essay "Violence and Metaphysics," a global negation of the sort that fascinates adolescents (such as "philosophy ended today," the assertion he explores at the beginning of the essay) is as impossible to prove as is a global affirmation. What is undermined in Derrida's work is the facile pretension to global knowledge. What is explored in deconstructive work, particularly in Derrida's work, are the tensions caused by our textual and social efforts to smuggle in externality, presence, totality (a term borrowed from Emmanuel Levinas).

Levinas's discussion of totality is a good place from which to consider this matter. With pretension to totality comes warfare, he says. With recognition of infinity comes peace. In either case, the motive for action comes from an encounter with difference, with an other. For a totalizing scheme, difference is a threat that must be conquered. For a totalizing scheme an unsubsumed other is a dissonance, the beginning of dissolution, a sign that everything is coming apart. The only stability that can be imagined in such a system is a stability imposed from without, from outside. And since the Outside is disturbingly reluctant to directly intervene to establish harmony, warfare is necessary for anyone who would do the work of God, the great Outside.

And so everything holds together because everything is *held* together. Now the heatedness of the discussion of deconstruction begins to make a bit more sense. From such a viewpoint, deconstruction is not an idea among other ideas, rather it represents the destruction of the possibility of having ideas and of making arguments. This would be serious business indeed.

But it is to be noted that Levinas does not imagine that infinity (the alternative to totality), is some sort of gentle, soft relativism, a lukewarm state of being in which there are no responsibilities, no duties, no justice possible. Quite to the contrary: for Levinas, the encounter with another is an encounter with infinity. The encounter with difference, particularly in the form of the face of the other (whom I cannot control or predict), gives rise, necessarily, to a powerful, and absolute, ethics. This is the other whom I must not kill. This may seem a small thing, too little to build ethics, justice, and stability on. But I was raised on Luther's Small Catechism, and thus am practiced in hearing an ever-expanding web of positive commands in a simple prohibition. "You shall not kill," says the commandment. "What does this mean?" asks Martin Luther, the catechist. "It means," he answers, "that we should fear and love God so that we do not endanger our neighbor's life, nor cause him any harm, but help and befriend him in every necessity of life." What starts as a pointed prohibition grows outward into a theological ethics of life with neighbors.

This same expanding crystallization of a small absolute is familiar to anyone who, like Levinas, is steeped in rabbinic interpretation. This is the other whom I must not kill. This may seem small, but Levinas draws from it both stability and justice.

A full consideration of the complications of Levinas's arguments would take more time than can be spent here. What is important to the present argument is the simple observation that Levinas, in rejecting externality of the sort usually insisted upon by those who guard against dissolution of thought and argument, argues for a stable and absolute ethics, a justice, and a kind of stabilizing externality that does not rely on presuming to act from an impossible standpoint. For Levinas, this externality comes, not despite the difference and difficulty of otherness, but precisely in human encounter with that difference and difficulty.

What is delightful about Derrida's exploration of Levinas's argument is the way he plays Levinas back against himself, the way he argues that even Levinas's construal of the world presupposes a kind of impossible external guarantee of stability, in that he does not adequately account for reciprocity in his sketch of the encounter with an other. This intensification of Levinas's insight is delightful because it does not bring incoherence, it does not undermine ethics; rather it intensifies also the absolute call to reciprocal answerability issued as a result of reciprocal encounters between mutually active Sames and Others.

Again, the complexities of this argument are sometimes dizzying. But still what rings through this is a discovery (and presupposition) of a kind of working, evolving, constantly negotiated (and therefore possible, in a sense that would make sense to Aristotle)[12] stability and reliability. Deconstruction practiced in this way is not a celebration of nihilism. It is an investigation of the protocols of stability in the midst of irreducible and shifting difference and multiplicity.[13]

Here recent work in culture-critical studies becomes especially valuable. Kathryn Tanner explores the implications of postmodernism for Christian theology and finds that stability and reliability are not only possible in the midst of shifting multiplicity, they are funded by it.[14] Brian Blount argues, analogously, that the cultural multiplicity that attends biblical interpretation provides the conditions for stability and reliability. Blount implies (helpfully and correctly, I think) that the real threat to validity to interpretation (to borrow a red herring from Eric D.

Hirsch)[15] comes from unilateral assertions of totality and adequacy.[16] Derrida (and Levinas) would, I think, agree.

What Is a Storyteller to Make of All This?

I think a storyteller is in a uniquely privileged position to make (at least provisional) sense of what might otherwise be an impossibly arcane argument. This is, first of all, because a storyteller, particularly one working as part of an ensemble, is responsible to embody the story that is being told. This requires finding all the possible physical sources of the words and actions reported in the story. This requires, in addition, negotiating each strategy for physical embodiment of the story with the other members of the ensemble, who are similarly engaged in physical exploration of the story. Levinas's encounter with the face of the other is the constant experience of a member of an ensemble responsible for telling a story. Derrida's sense of ethical and metaphysical reciprocity, and of the responsibility they imply, bubbles up through any attempt to tell any story.

Storytellers discover, again and again and inescapably, that externality comes into the story in the body of the others, incarnated reciprocally (as it were) in the risks and difficulties implied by the reality of the face-to-face encounter that ensemble storytelling makes necessary. Perhaps Christianity is an inherently unstable theology (Jewish colleagues point this out with some regularity), but it is to be noted that Christians achieve such stability and reliability as are possible by establishing reference to the Incarnation of Externality in Jesus. This makes the matter of re-membering Jesus even more crucial (note the word) than it seemed when first we encountered the notion in chapter 1.

Second, storytellers are in a position to make working sense of deconstructive work because of the implications of intertextuality, because of the ways and reasons that stories stick to other stories. An attentive storyteller will notice when a gospel narrative has stuck itself onto an action-adventure movie like "Conan the Barbarian." She will even experiment to see what happens when a gospel is played as such a movie. An attentive storyteller will also notice when the story she is telling has shifted its adhesive allegiances to yet another story, yet another structure of conspiracy and expectation. She will notice, for instance, if Jesus is no longer being read, intertextually, as a warrior. Above all, an attentive storyteller will discover that, if stories create worlds (as argued in chapter 1) and if stories of all sorts hold tight to each other, then when these stories and worlds begin to come apart, they do that together, as well. At the point where cultural narratives begin not to work, gospel narratives (which are also cultural narratives) will also show signs of breakdown. This will be true even for those Christians who have sought to practice their faith in a self-imposed cultural vacuum. That means that an attentive storyteller, one who notices when she and audiences are using a different intertext to make sense of the story she is telling, is in possession of a valuable diagnostic sign, a key to the forces working in the culture of which she and her audience are a part.

Which means that any reading strategy that tries to do its work in isolation from other cultural stories (whether the isolation is intentional or accidental to another principle of operation) will misunderstand the problems it encounters. The problems faced by other narratives in the culture will infiltrate the interpretive process, damaging reading structures and cutting lines of communication without being noticed. This leads to flawed interpretations, and useless tellings of the stories.

Which means that storytellers need to adopt the discipline of exploring all the cultural narratives they can find. They need to ride the narrative bus, so to speak. They need to sit in bars and watch stories dance and link up with each other. They need to cultivate the habit of watching the ways secular stories and biblical stories shape each other reciprocally. Jesus may have taken his disciples up a high mountain, alone and set apart, but that must not be taken to imply that the tellers of gospel stories ought similarly to retreat from all the other stories that surround them. They will not be successful. Instead, they will find themselves with an entire truckload of stories whose existence they do not acknowledge.

Which means that storytellers, to practice their craft responsibly, must develop the discipline of watching their audiences carefully because audiences shift intertextual allegiances all the time. Audiences sometimes hear things that mortify the teller of the story. Sometimes it's because the audience listens poorly. Sometimes it's because the teller does her job poorly. Often it's because of the power of the intertextual web of stories and structures that shape the way we tell and the way we listen. A storyteller has to learn to watch for this, and to make allowances for this. A responsible storyteller has to learn where audiences are likely to go, given the opportunity, and to find ways to reshape their hearing. It is not easy, or certain. Stories hold together with each other with such force that they can take apart almost any telling. A storyteller has to remember that.

Storytellers also need to play with the ways stories hold together and come apart. They need to organize dances between stories that audiences never imagined would even talk together. Strange things happen when you do. Strange and productive things. Sometimes an audience will react to the dance and pull back from the intertextual reading, which is useful when the cross-text is venomous. Sometimes an audience will tumble together with the intertextual reading and find a way of hearing and telling and reading that is new, surprising, and insightful. And sometimes an audience will discover, as they listen to an unfamiliar crossing of texts, that the cross-text reveals what their own reading practice has been all along. They just didn't know it. The conservative Christians in my class were quite surprised to discover that they were reading Jesus as Conan the Barbarian. Some were not particularly pleased. Others were thrilled. All of them rethought their own reading practice when they discovered how the story held together and came apart.

The intertextual power of the audience to hear a story differently and to reshape its meaning shows up any time old stories are being told, especially old, familiar stories. For instance, consider the experience of reading and telling and hearing the story of Cinderella. There are a great many things to be found in this old story, some of them the same basic human tensions that have been felt in the story for generations. The central character struggles against abandonment and abuse. True quality finally shines through despite attempts to hide it under ashes and rags. And, at least in the old original, not yet sanitized and weakened, evil-doing is punished. The proper order of things is reasserted.[17]

There is also, however, a problem in the story that has been felt more intensely in recent years: the story resolves a young woman's problem by attaching her to a prince. There certainly are many positive readings possible, perhaps even of the use made of relationality in the plot of this old story. According to such a reading the tension in the story is resolved when, in the end, a human alliance (between the prince and

Cinderella) defeats inhuman abuse. There may be many other positive readings imaginable, but at the end of all attempts to read this story positively and unambiguously, there will always remain a problem for contemporary tellers and audiences who no longer imagine that a woman has no problems that cannot be solved by belonging to a man. As it says on an old bumper sticker: A Woman without a Man Is Like a Fish without a Bicycle.

Old stories often have this problem. When they were told in earlier days, to other audiences, they were told in the midst of worlds that no longer exist, at least not in the same form. Presuppositions change, and so do our predispositions, and when they change, we find ourselves sticking to different things in stories we have heard and heard and heard. Different things hold the story together, and different things make the telling fall apart. When Rodgers and Hammerstein retold this old story in the 1960s the issue was whether a "plain country bumpkin and a prince could join in marriage." Impossible. But, of course (as the song concludes), "impossible things are happening every day." And, indeed, they were in the United States in those days after two wars and one "police action" and in the beginning of the slide into another. And, indeed, in those days when the country was still being stirred and mixed by the increasing postwar migration of plain country bumpkins into urban areas, this story will (at least in part) begin to be a story about the new possibility that even a childhood in the agrarian hinterland could be escaped and forgotten, a positive outcome, at least for those who desired it.

Different audiences hear different things in the old stories. But contemporary audiences will often hear something disturbing in the Cinderella story, no matter how it fits into the social history of this, or any other, country. What does it mean to tell our daughters (and sons) stories that imply that no woman is complete until she is safely reattached to a male protector? Good question. The answers given by general audiences to this question have changed over the years. And when audiences change, the story changes.

Indeed, the American audience was already changing when Rodgers and Hammerstein's *Cinderella* was first telecast, as may be heard in James Thurber's retelling of the story of Red Riding Hood.[18] In Thurber's version, there is still a wolf, a girl, and a grandmother, but now the girl has no need to wait for a trusty woodsman to arrive to save the day. When the wolf approaches, the girl pulls a .45 out of her basket and blows the wolf away. The moral of the story? As Thurber says, "It isn't so easy to fool little girls nowadays as it once was."[19] Indeed it is not, and thank goodness, so says (one must assume) the general audience to this old story. The audience has changed, and with it the story and also the teller.

PART TWO:
HOW TO DISCOVER HOW STORIES HOLD TOGETHER AND COME APART

Pick a Story

Here's another set of suggested stories to explore. As always, there are many other stories that you could choose. These have the advantage of provoking thought about how stories come apart and hold together. I call them cross-woven stories:

Storm in a Boat (Mk. 4:35–41) crossed with When It Came To Be the Sixth Hour (Mk. 15:33–39);

Rachel Weeping for Her Children (Matt. 2:13–18) crossed with From the Sixth Hour On (Matt. 27:38–56), perhaps also crossed with an episode from, for instance, Elie Wiesel's *Night*.

Warm Up

By now, perhaps you and your gathered group have grown accustomed to physical preparation for interpretation. Even after you reach that stage, warm-up will still seem strange. And, as I have said before, that is because it *is* strange. Do it anyway. Feel free to move beyond the basic exercises that have been suggested here, and don't worry about picking the *best* warm-up exercises. Remember, there are no such exercises. With practice you will develop a sense of what a specific exercise is likely to contribute to your work, but even then do not spend too much time agonizing over which exercise would be perfect. The thing that is essential and perfect is the physical warm-up itself. Do that and don't worry too much about the rest. Accept serendipity when it surprises you.

Do a Read-Around and a Gesture-Around

By now the Read-Around is likely to work fairly well for your group. The Gesture-Around will take longer to ripen, I expect. The texts suggested for this chapter will pose new problems for both activities. It is to be hoped that these are productive problems.

There are many ways to do a Cross-Woven text. You can simply read one text and then read the other. You can have two players read the texts simultaneously. Or you can interweave the lines from the two texts and make a cross-woven whole. This last possibility is, in my experience, the strongest way to go. But it is the most difficult. Use the Read-Around as the time to draw your group into this act of collaborative creation.

First, do a Read-Around for each text separately. Gather what has been seen and heard. Look for gestures and postures that seem required by each text. As your group works with the texts, listen for hooks that might serve to link the two texts together. Encourage them to do the same.

Now gather suggestions from the group about how the two texts might be woven into each other. Set this as an exercise in making productive mistakes, and be careful to maintain an environment that makes it safe to take risks. Some of the suggestions that arise will be unworkable. Be especially thankful for those suggestions. Try them anyway. You might be quite wrong about what will, and will not, work.

This process will usually take several tries; it might even take several sessions, but the result can be remarkable. It all starts in the Read-Around.

Now comes the Gesture-Around. Because one of the tasks of this session is the crossing of disparate texts, you might want to spend some time as a group watching old movies from easily identifiable genres. Watch old mysteries, old detective movies, old screwball comedies; watch kung-fu movies. What you are looking for are gestures, postures, and ways of speaking that you can use in the scenes you will be developing. For now, try to use any identified gestures in your Gesture-Around. If you discover stock gestural vocabularies that go with different kinds of stories, it will be quite useful.

Attempt Some First Embodiments

Developing embodiments of these stories takes a lot of practice. It will be some time before your scenes are particularly pleasing. Keep at it. It is worth the effort.

For now, the task remains largely the same, as it will for the foreseeable future. Your goal is to develop more facility and more subtlety in your embodied scenes. Your goal is to gain clarity about how external linkages shape the story we thought we knew. And, your goal is to gain awareness of the inescapable deformation that goes with interpretation of any text, no matter the method.

In this session, your goal expands to include also the development of those abilities and understandings that will allow you and your group to weave some stories together and present the cross-woven result in a form that will make sense to an audience. You are after coherence. Coherence is not found by denying the moments of fragmentation and tension that you have found in the texts you have worked with. On the contrary, coherence is found through exploration of those moments, through discovery of how the text works to make sense. In the "why-to" section of this chapter, considerable time was spent looking at the ways context, intratext, and intertext hold texts together. Now that you've reached the "how-to" section, you will benefit most if you use your group worksession to explore these matters further. The cross-woven texts suggested previously will allow you to experiment with the working of intra- and intertextuality. You might also go back to stories you've worked with before and play them in a fuller context, just to see what the context does for the coherence of the story.

Here's a hint: look at what happens as soon as Jesus finishes the scene with the Syrophoenician woman in the gospel of Mark. Commentators have noted that his travels in the next verse or so would take far longer than the time apparently allotted. This has led to commentators making the assumption that Mark just didn't know his map very well. Maybe, as a context, this spinning, racing journey is instead to be taken as Jesus beating a hasty retreat. That contextual possibility would create all sorts of productive difficulty. Remember: context can destabilize as well as it can stabilize the meaning of the story.

Necessary Multiplicity

As your scenes get better and more polished, it becomes more tempting to abandon your earlier commitment to playing everything several ways. Resist this temptation with all your might. You have not been playing these scenes over and over, different way after different way, just because the first efforts at this way of working are usually not so good. You have been playing these scenes multiple ways because multiplicity is necessary. If your aim is to crack open these old stories, to move beyond the standard-issue readings that everyone knows, the only way to do that is to keep moving beyond what you have already done. As soon as you stop and freeze the way you are doing a story, you make it into a new standard-issue reading of the story, and it will become as dusty as any of the old dusty readings. The better your scenes get, the more important it is to maintain the flexibility and freedom needed to leave them behind. Practice this. It is hard work. Remember, magnificent failures are the air you breathe when you work with texts this way.

Homework

In previous chapters I've sent you to the theater and to movies for your homework. That's still a good assignment. There is plenty there to be learned. This time, however, look for movies that follow identifiable formulas. For your homework, expand on the work you began when you were working on the Gesture-Around. Find some classic movies and watch them. Chart the plots. How is tension created in such movies? How is it released? How do you recognize the good guys and the bad guys? Are there gestures, postures, or ways of speaking that give away such information? Is there a gestural vocabulary tied to the movies you are watching?

If you want to see a truly odd movie that will help you think about gestural vocabularies, find the movie *Jesus Christ, Vampire Hunter*. Yes, this movie is exactly as strange as it sounds. And no, you might very well not want to develop scenes that look anything like this movie. But the movie takes an easily recognizable genre and imposes it on an extremely well-known character. The result is strange, sometimes hilarious, always surprising, frequently simply bizarre. The value of watching such a movie is that, after *Jesus Christ, Vampire Hunter*, your strangest scenes will seem pretty middle of the road.

Suggested Reading

Aristotle, *The Rhetoric and the Poetics of Aristotle*. New York: Random House, 1984.

Bettelheim, Bruno. *The Uses of Enchantment: The Meaning and Importance of Fairy Tales*. New York: Vintage Books, 1977.

Blount, Brian. *Cultural Interpretation: Reorienting New Testament Criticism.* Minneapolis: Fortress, 1995.

Pinkola, Clarissa Estes. *Women Who Run With Wolves: Myths and Stories of the Wild Woman Archetype.* New York: Ballantine, 1992.

Silko, Leslie Marmon. *Storyteller.* New York: Arcade, 1981.

Steiner, George. *Real Presences.* Chicago: University of Chicago, 1989.

Tanner, Kathryn. *Theories of Culture: A New Agenda for Theology.* Minneapolis: Fortress, 1997.

Thurber, James. *Fables for Our Times.* New York: Harper, 1940.

5

Conclusion: Provoking the Gospel

At the beginning of the book I talked about this necessity of taking risks in biblical interpretation. In chapter after chapter you have had a chance to take some of those risks, to make some productive mistakes. So far, I'm guessing, most of the risks have been small, most of the mistakes have been minor ones, and most of the gain has been slight. That is the way it starts.

Throughout the chapters I have directed you (repeatedly, to say the least) to pay careful attention, both to the people and to the process I have been laying out. I have asked you to ask the members of your group what they saw and what they heard, and I have told you (again, repeatedly) to honor what they noticed, however trivial it may have seemed. I have also directed you to be careful to honor your group, to honor especially your outsiders and your audiences. I suspect those directions were ones you did not need, mostly. I would like to take this opportunity to thank you for your patient endurance. As Woody Guthrie used to say, "Just think of me as someone who told you something you already knew."

I have spent so much time on these matters because you are engaged in a process (still very much in the beginning stages) of stretching out a space in which you and your group will be able to work. More particularly, you are working to create a space in which it will be safe to make mistakes. Having already devoted a whole chapter to the matter of making mistakes, it surely seems like overkill to return to this issue again. Maybe it is overkill, but it is also crucial.

Risks and mistakes are central to this way of working with biblical stories. That will surely be true because of the demands of performance. Painful self-consciousness makes for dull performance. Your players will surely need the freedom to take risks in performance if they are ever going to be worth looking at when they play these stories for an audience. But that is not the main reason why it is so important to create a safe place in which to make mistakes and take risks. The main reason is that some of the things that actually provoke the gospel will feel like a terrible mistake when they occur to members of your group. We use religion as an occasion to repeat platitudes and to tell ourselves that everything is okay. Such utterances always feel safe and right. And they often are both safe and right. But the provocations that you are after, the ones that call out the gospel in its most vigorous form, will feel neither safe nor right to the members of your group when they run into them. And if you have not carefully created a space, stretched it out, that allows such frightening provocations to be tried out, then you will miss the very thing that links biblical stories to real physical life and actual audiences. Back in the introduction I told you the story of my experience teaching creation stories to undergraduates. I told you especially about the discovery I made when I had some of my storytellers (both skilled actors) play the Marduk and Tiamat story for the members of my class. I have not yet told you the crucial part of that story.

That way of working was surely a valuable teaching tool. It surprised the members of the class (violence is always shocking) and cracked open a story that is often hard to teach effectively. It ought to be noted (and it may have occurred to you) that this is an awfully long and dangerous way to go for a teaching tool. If the only goal and only outcome of playing the Marduk and Tiamat story was to rub the students' noses in the graphic violence of the story, there would have been safer, and wiser, ways to do it.

There is something more here, something beyond just a teaching tool, something that showed up in several notes sent to me by members of the class (some of them anonymously) after we had worked through the issues raised by these opposing creation stories and after we had performed our work for an audience. Several women in the class wrote to me to thank me for the work we had done together on creation stories, particularly on the ways Genesis 2 resists and seeks to heal the violence of the Marduk and Tiamat story. "I was Tiamat for a while in high school," said one particularly strong young woman. "I was beaten and abused as a child," said one. "My father was Marduk," said another. Another person, writing anonymously, described the process of creating and performing the scene as "incredibly healing."

If it had been only a single note, an isolated response, still it would have been worth the risk. But it was several people, and when they performed the scene for the public you could feel in the room the same physical tension. Clearly, there were several more people who had lived the story we played and knew the risks and dangers firsthand. In that setting, the creation story in Genesis 2 entered the room as a true story of resistance, a story of the creation of life in direct opposition to death.

The text, the process, the risks (taken in a safe space), and the physical reality of the performance all conspired together to provoke the gospel. This is why the risks are justified. This is why the hard work of developing a group is worth taking on. This is why the odd warm-up exercises are worth doing. This is why it is worthwhile to play these scenes again and again, even when nothing much is happening yet. In the experience of my storytelling team, something will happen. In fact, something is happening already. You just have to wait for it.

And you have to keep poking at the stories, provoking them. You have to learn to love being poked back and provoked. Out of this process the gospel gets provoked and called out into the open. When that happens it will change you, your group, and your audience. It will be worth the wait. Turlough O'Carolan, blind harper and last of the Irish bards, is reported to have asked, "Tell me this, man: Which do you think is harder: to make dark songs in the darkness or to make brilliant ones that shine through the gloom?" May you learn to provoke the gospel and may your songs shine.

APPENDIX

(Please feel free to photocopy these texts for your own use.)

Bread in a Boat
Mark 8:14–21

> They had forgot to bring bread.
>> They had only one loaf with them in the boat.
>> Jesus was commanding them:
>>> Watch out.
>>> Beware of the leaven of the Pharisees
>>>> and the leaven of Herod.
>> They were saying to each other:
>>> It's because we don't have any bread.
>> When he realized what they were doing,
>>> he says to them:
>>>> Why are you saying:
>>>>> It's because we don't have any bread?
>>>> Don't you get it?
>>>> Do you really not understand?
>>>>> How thick are your skulls, anyway?
>>>> You have eyes, and you can't see?
>>>> Ears you have, but you can't hear?
>>>> Nobody remembers?
>>>>> When I broke five loaves for 5000 people,
>>>>> how many baskets of leftovers did you pick up?

They say to him:
    Twelve.
        And the seven loaves for the 4000?
        How many baskets of leftovers did you pick up?
They say:
    Seven.
He kept saying to them:
    You don't get it yet, do you?

And Throw It to the Dogs
Mark 7:24–30

He went up from there,
    away into the region of Tyre.
He went into a house,
    he wanted no one to know.
        There was no hiding him.
A woman heard about him,
    a woman whose daughter had an unclean spirit.
        She came.
        She fell at his feet.
            The woman was a Gentile,
                Syrophoenician by birth.
        She asked him to cast the demon out of her daughter.
He tried to say to her:
    Let the children be fed first,
        for it is not right to take the children's bread
        and throw it to the dogs.
But she answered,
    says to him, she does:
        Sir, even the dogs under the table eat the children's
        bread crumbs.
And he said to her:
    Because of this word, go,
    the demon has come out of your daughter.

And after she went into her house,
    she found the child thrown upon the bed,
    the demon gone.

Now the Snake Was the Cleverest

Genesis 3:1–7

(This translation is based on the work of Everett Fox and Mary Phil Korsak, which was based on the translation of Martin Buber and Franz Rosenzweig.)

Now the snake was more clever
    more clever than all the living-things of the field that the LORD
    God had made.
It said to the woman:
    So God said: You are not to eat from any of the trees
    in the garden . . . !
The woman said to the snake:
    From the fruit of the (other) trees in the garden we may eat,
        but from the fruit of the tree that is in the midst of the garden,
    God has said:
        You are not to eat from it and you are not to touch it,
            lest you die.
The snake said to the woman:
    Die, you will not die!
    No, God knows
        that on the day that you eat from it, your eyes will be opened
        and you will become like God, knowing good and bad.
The woman saw
    that the tree was good for eating
    and that it was a delight to the eyes,
    and the tree was desirable to contemplate.
She took from its fruit and ate
    and gave also to her man beside her, and he ate.
The eyes of the two of them were opened
    and they knew
    that they were naked.
They sewed fig leaves together and made themselves loincloths.

He Is Coming Up Out of the Water
Mark 1:4–11

John appeared,
    John the Baptist,
    appeared in the wilderness,
proclaiming a baptism of repentance
    aiming at forgiveness of sins.
All the region of Judea was going out to him,
    all that region
    and every person living in Jerusalem.
They were being baptized by him in the Jordan river,
    baptized while they confessed their sins.
        John was clothed in camel hair.
        He had a leather belt around his waist.
        He ate locusts and wild honey.
John proclaimed:
    He is coming,
        the one who is stronger than I,
    he is coming after me.
    I am not worthy to stoop down to untie the thong of his sandals.
    I baptized you with water.
        He, however, will baptize you in holy spirit.
It happened in those days:
    Jesus came from Nazareth of Galilee
        and was baptized in the Jordan by John.
    He is coming up out of the water
        and BANG he sees the heavens being torn apart
            and the spirit,
                like a pigeon,
    coming down into him.
A voice came out of the heavens:
    You are my son, the beloved.
        With you I am well pleased.

River of Blood
Mark 5:21–43

When Jesus departed in the boat back to the other shore,
a huge a crowd came together upon him.
He was by the sea.
    A person came to him,
        one of the leaders of the synagogue,
        his name was Jairus.
    When he saw Jesus,
    he fell at his feet;
    he begged him desperately:
        My daughter is at the point of death.
        Come and lay your hands upon her.
    Jesus went with him.
        A crowd followed him,
        a crowd so large that it crushed him.
A woman came,
    a woman twelve years in a river of blood,
        twelve years having suffered many things
        under many healers,
    a woman who had exhausted all her property,
        all her substance,
        after twelve years she had improved not at all,
            in fact, her condition had grown worse.
    A woman came into the area,
        came because she had heard about Jesus.
    This woman came into the crowd behind Jesus
        and touched his clothing.
        She was saying:
            even if I only touch the hem of his garment,
                I will be rescued.
    BANG the spring of her blood was dried up
        and she knew in her body
        that she was healed from her scourge.
    BANG Jesus knew in himself
        that power had gone out from him.

Turning and turning, around in the crowd,
    he kept saying:
        Who touched my clothing?
    His disciples were saying to him:
        You can see the crowd crushing you
        and you say: Who touched me?
He kept looking around
    to find the woman who had done this.
The woman,
    afraid and trembling,
knew what had happened to her.
The woman came and fell down before him.
She told him the whole truth.
He said to her:
    Daughter, your faithfulness has saved you.
    Depart in peace
and be healed from your scourge.
While he was still speaking
they came to him from the leader of the synagogue:
    Your daughter has died, they said,
    why bother the teacher any longer?
Jesus overheard what they were saying.
He says to the leader of the synagogue:
    Do not fear, only be faithful.
He would not allow anyone to be with him,
    no one except Peter, James, and John
        (the brother of James).
They come into the house of the leader of the synagogue.
He sees an uproar:
    everywhere wild wailing,
    everywhere shrieking,
    everywhere howling.
He goes in and says to them:
    Why are you wailing?
    Why the uproar?
        The child has not died, she's only asleep.

They laughed at him bitterly.
He throws everyone out.
He takes the father of the child,
    the father and the mother,
    and those with him.
He goes into where the child was.
He grasps the hand of the child.
    He says to her:
      Talitha cum
        (translated: Little girl, I say to you, get up).
BANG the little girl rose and walked around
    (she was, after all, twelve years old).
BANG: ecstasy beyond ecstasy.
He strictly ordered them
    that no one should ever find out what had happened.
He told them to give her something to eat.

Sinks-Like-a . . .

Matthew 14:22–33

And BANG he made the disciples get into the boat
and go ahead of him to the other shore
    until he should release the crowds.
After he released the crowds he went up into the hills all alone
and prayed.
When it was evening he was there alone.
    The boat was already many stadia away from land,
      battered by the waves,
      for the wind was against it.
    In the fourth watch of the night
      he came toward them
        walking on the sea.
When the disciples saw him walking on the sea they were terrified.
    They said: It is a phantom,
      and they screamed from fear.

BANG Jesus spoke to them,
    he said: Have courage,
        I am,
        stop being afraid.
Peter answered him,
    he said: Lord,
        if you are you,
        order me to come toward you
            on the water.
Jesus said: come.
After he got out of the boat
    Peter walked
    on the water
    and came toward Jesus.
When he glanced at the wind he was afraid
    After he began to sink
        he screamed,
        he said: Lord, save me.
BANG Jesus reached out his hand
    he grabbed him
    he says to him:
        Little Faith,
        what was the point of doubting??
When they got back into the boat, the wind ceased.
Those in the boat worshiped him,
    they said: Truly you are the son of God.

Trees Walking
Mark 8:22–26

They went into Bethsaida.
They brought to him a blind man and asked him to touch him.
    He took the blind man by the hand
        and brought him out of the village.
    He spat into his eyes and placed his hands upon him,
        and then he asked him:
            Do you see anything?
    The man looked carefully and said:
        I see people,
        because I see them like trees that are walking.
Then Jesus placed his hands on his eyes again,
and the man looked hard,
and his sight was restored,
    he saw everything clearly.
Jesus sent him into his house and said:
    Don't even go into the village.

Who Is My Mother?
Matthew 12:46–50

While he was still speaking to the crowds,
    Look!
    his mother and his brothers were standing outside,
        seeking to speak with him.
    Someone said to him:
        Look! your mother and your brothers are standing outside
        seeking to speak with you.
    Jesus answered,
        he said to the one who talked to him:
            Who is my mother?
        Who are my brothers?
    And reaching out his hand on his disciples
        he said: Look! My mother and my brothers.

For whoever should do the will of my father
    (my father in heaven)
he is my brother
and sister
and mother.

Storm in a Boat
Mark 4:35–41

On that day when it was evening, he says to them:
    Let's go across to the other side.
So they leave the crowd and take him,
    since he was already in the boat.
        Other boats were with him.
A great windstorm arises;
    the waves beat into the boat,
    the boat is being swamped.
        He was in the stern,
            his head on the pillow,
            sound asleep.
They wake him up and say to him:
    Teacher, does it not matter to you that we are dying?
        He woke up;
        he rebuked the wind
        and he said to the sea:
            Silence. Be still.
The wind stopped. There was a dead calm.
He said to them:
    Why are you afraid like this?
    How do you not have faith?
And they feared a great fear,
    and they were saying to each other:
    Who is this guy? Even the wind and the sea obey him.

When It Came To Be the Sixth Hour
Mark 15:33–39

When it came to be the sixth hour, darkness came upon the whole
earth until the ninth hour,
    and in the ninth hour Jesus bellowed in a great voice:
        eloi eloi lema sabachthani
            (translated: My God, my God, why have you forsaken me?)
    Some of those standing by
        when they heard him,
    were saying:
        Look!
        He's calling Elijah.
   Someone ran and filled a sponge with sour wine,
        put it on a stick,
        and gave it to him to drink. saying:
            Wait,
            let's see whether Elijah will come to take him down.
    Jesus let loose a loud cry
        and breathed his last.
And the curtain of the Temple was ripped in two,
    from the top to the bottom.
But when the centurion,
    standing by opposite him,
saw that thus he breathed his last, he said:
    No doubt: If ever there was a son of God, he was it.

Rachel Weeping for Her Children
Matthew 2:13–18

After they had departed,
    look,
    a messenger of the LORD appears in a dream to Joseph
        saying: Get up,
            take the child and his mother
            and flee into Egypt

and be there until I should speak to you.
>For Herod is about to seek the child in order to kill him.
He got up
>took the child and his mother during the night
>>and departed into Egypt,
and he was there until the end of Herod
>in order that the word might be fulfilled,
>>the word from the Lord,
>>the word through the prophet
>>>which says: Out of Egypt I called my son.
Then Herod saw that he was ridiculed by the Magi.
>He was furious.
>He sent
>he killed all the children in Bethlehem and in all her region,
>>all the children from two years old and down,
>>>according to the time which he had discovered from
>>>the Magi.
Then was fulfilled the word through Jeremiah the prophet
which says:
>A voice in Ramah is heard,
>>wailing and great mourning,
>Rachel shrieking for her children,
>>and she will not be comforted:
>they are not.

From the Sixth Hour On
Matthew 27:38–56

Then they crucified with him two bandits,
>one on his right
>and one on his left.
Those passing by blasphemed him
>wagging their heads and saying,
>>The destroyer of the Temple,
>>The one who will rebuild it in three days,
>save yourself,

since you are the son of God,
come down from the cross.
Likewise even the high priests
mocking him together with the scribes and the elders
were saying:
Others he saved,
himself he is not able to save.
He is the king of Israel,
let him come down now from the cross
and we will be faithful to him.
He has trusted on God,
let God deliver him now,
if he wants him.
For he said
"I am the son of God."
Even the bandits crucified with him gave him the same insult.
From the sixth hour darkness was upon all the earth up until
the ninth hour.
Around the ninth hour Jesus bellowed in a great voice,
he says: *Eli, Eli, lema sabachthani?*
Which is: My God, my God, to what end have you
abandoned me?
After some of those standing there heard him,
they were saying:
this guy is calling Elijah.
And BANG one of them ran
and taking a sponge
he filled it with vinegar
and placing it on a reed
he gave it to him to drink.
The others were saying:
Wait, let us see if Elijah is coming to save him.
Jesus,
again shrieking in a great voice,
released his breath.
And, look, the curtain of the Temple was torn
from above to below

into two pieces,
and the earth shook,
and the rocks were ripped.
The tombs were opened
   and many bodies of holy ones who had died were raised
   They went out of their tombs
     after his resurrection
   and went into the holy city
   and were seen by many.
The centurion
  and those with him guarding Jesus
    when they saw the earthquake and the things that happened
were terribly afraid
  They said Truly this one was the son of God.
There were many women there
  watching from a distance,
    women who had followed Jesus from Galilee to deacon to him.
      Among them were Mary Magdalene
      and Mary the mother of James and Joseph
      and the mother of the sons of Zebedee.

NOTES

PREFACE

1. Shimon Levy, *The Bible as Theatre* (Brighton: Sussex Academic Press, 2000), ix.

2. The way this scripture identifies Isaac, of course, completely ignores Ishmael, Abraham's first son. This rather surprising omission must also poke and provoke us.

INTRODUCTION

1. The emphasis on skill at this point is crucial. Do not attempt this unless you have people trained in stage combat. Such a scene can be physically dangerous and emotionally terrifying. Select your actors well and carefully.

1. RE-MEMBERING THE STORY

1. Kermode's full discussion is worth reading. You can find it in his *The Sense of an Ending: Studies in the Theory of Fiction* (London: Oxford University Press, 1967), 39. He writes, "Myths are the agents of stability, fictions are the agents of change."

2. One of the best, and most engaging, discussions of this matter is to be found in Annie Dillard, *Living By Fiction* (New York: Harper & Row, 1982).

3. Plato's *Gorgias* is good reading on this point. Gorgias presents himself as a teacher of public argumentation. By this he means that he teaches people how to persuade other people about matters of what is right or wrong. Along the way he admits that he merely creates *opinion* about what is right or wrong, not actual knowledge of anything. This admission is telling.

4. Aristotle, *Poetics*, 1450b30, 1451b1, 1451b6, (McGraw-Hill, 1984).

5. Mark 8:31, for example.

6. The best resource for this is Donald Juel, *Messianic Exegesis* (Philadelphia: Fortress, 1988). See also Nils Dahl, "The Crucified Messiah," collected in *Jesus the Christ: The Historical Origins of Christological Doctrine,* ed. Donald Juel (Minneapolis: Fortress, 1991).

7. This is, perhaps, best illustrated by the badly rendered picture of a crucified ass with a figure kneeling before it, worshiping his god.

8. 1 Corinthians 1:23. The word μωρια (*moria*) is generally translated as "folly" or "foolishness," which captures neither the harsh force of the word nor the social impact that crucifixion seems to have had. English needs a word that means "moronicness" to capture the sense of μωρια.

9. See Umberto Eco's *Six Walks in the Fictional Woods* (Cambridge: Harvard University Press, 1994) for a good, accessible introduction to this matter.

10. "Der Herd der Feindschaft gegen Jesus" in the original German. Ernst Lohmeyer, *Galiläa und Jerusalem* (Göttingen: Vandenhoeck & Ruprecht, 1936), 32.

11. Irenaeus, Adv. Haer. 3.11.8: "It is not possible that the Gospels can be either more or fewer in number than they are. For, since there are

four zones of the world in which we live, and four principal winds, while the Church is scattered throughout all the world, and the 'pillar and ground' of the Church is the Gospel and the spirit of life; it is fitting that she should have four pillars, breathing out immortality on every side, and vivifying men afresh."

12. One hears this kind of condescending approach to the ancient world, and to cultures judged to be "primitive," in studies written in the late nineteenth and early twentieth centuries. See the analyses of this phenomenon in Brian Swann, ed., *Smoothing the Ground: Essays on Native American Oral Literature* (Berkeley: University of California Press, 1983).

13. Robert W. Funk and Roy W. Hoover, eds., *The Five Gospels* (San Francisco: HarperSanFrancisco, 1993), 502.

14. Funk and Hoover, *Five Gospels*, 501.

15. This is "a motif repeated elsewhere in Thomas (in the parable of the leaven, Thomas 96·1–2, and in the parable of the fishnet, 8:1–3)." Funk and Hoover, *Five Gospels*, 529.

16. One particularly interesting guess about Thomas and its form is that items on the list were meant to be plugged into a larger narrative, which was the secret possession of the community.

17. The most entertaining, and insightful, exploration of this phenomenon is to be found in Stanley Fish's *Is There a Text in This Class?: The Authority of Interpretive Communities* (Cambridge: Harvard University Press, 1980). Because texts exist only as they are read, to talk about the borders of the community is also to talk about the edges of the text.

18. There are many useful introductions to this notion. Perhaps the best is to be found in Wayne Booth's *The Rhetoric of Fiction* (Chicago: University of Chicago Press, 1983). See especially his opening discussion of "telling and showing," 3–22. It's also worth noting that television soap operas provide easy demonstration of the way a reader/viewer is maneuvered onto the constructed platform. The ideology of the story is imposed quite powerfully in that particular genre.

19. See Wolfgang Iser, *The Fictive and the Imaginary: Charting Literary Anthropology* (Baltimore: Johns Hopkins University Press, 1993). See also his earlier work, *Prospecting: From Reader Response to Literary Anthropology* (Baltimore: Johns Hopkins University Press, 1989).

20. See Booth's discussion of this scene in "Rabelais and Feminist Criticism" in *The Company We Keep: An Ethics of Fiction* (Berkeley: University of California Press, 1988), 382–418.

21. Jane Tompkins, *West of Everything: The Inner Life of Westerns* (Oxford: Oxford University Press, 1992), 228.

22. Ibid., 233.

23. Thomas Boomershine, *Story Journey: An Invitation to the Gospel as Storytelling* (Nashville: Abingdon, 1988), 44.

24. This is the physical implication of the verb, splagcnizomai in Mark 1:41.

25. See the translations of this passage in the NRSV and the TEV, which have Jesus moved or filled with pity, a particularly weak word in common American usage, in any case.

26. Mark 1:43, NEB.

27. Mark 8:30, NEB.

2. TAKING PLACE . . . TAKING UP SPACE

1. For a fascinating exploration of the twists and turns of translation, see Douglas R. Hofstadter's *Le Ton beau de Marot: In Praise of the Music of Language* (New York: Basic Books, 1997).

2. The notion of the existence of an "other one" that needs properly to be referred to with a capital letter has a long and fascinating history. Back behind this notion stand a great many thinkers, movements, solutions, and problems. Somewhere in the background you will find Rudolf Otto and the "Wholly Other," who was also the "Holy Other." Somewhere in the background you will also find Martin Buber addressing a "Thou." Nearer to our time and to the drive of the present discussion, of course, is the more recent work of Emmanuel Levinas. His *Totality and Infinity: An Essay on Exteriority* (Pittsburgh: Duquesne University Press, 1969) makes good, if difficult, reading at this point.

3. "The laws of movement govern all theatrical situations." Jacques Lecoq, *The Moving Body: Teaching Creative Theatre* (New York: Routledge, 2001; first published in French as *Le corps poetique,* Actes Sud-Papiers, 1997), 21.

4. Here see Lecoq's opinion of the impact of self-expression on theatrical process: "Unfortunately many people enjoy expressing themselves . . . forgetting that . . . spectators must receive pleasure." *Moving Body,* 18.

5. Lecoq, *Moving Body*, 139–40.

6. To rediscover the importance of this historical, cultural, and archaeological investigation, you might want to reread the flurry of responses to the publication of a computer-generated image of what Jesus may have looked like. Needless to say, the image did not look much like Sallman's head of Christ or like any Sunday school picture of Jesus. Particularly instructive was the reaction Kathleen Parker presented in her syndicated column in April of 2001. She objects to the alteration of our image of Jesus in the same breath, and for the same reasons, as she objects to the changing image of Betty Crocker. "Jeez Louise," she complains, "can't we have a holiday without iconoclasm?" Her sentiment might be understandable, but her linking of Jesus to the advertising icon, Betty Crocker, is telling. There never was a historical Betty Crocker. She was from the start an advertising icon. For Parker, and perhaps for the reacting public, there never should have been a historical Jesus, only an iconic one who must remain divinely unchanging once he's been made into a logo for God as we care to think about him. Such rather chilling notions will drive even the most determined literary interpreter to historical study in a flash.

7. This translation, obviously atypical, attempts to catch the force of the unusual word that is usually translated as "of Nazareth." The form of the word is not quite correct if the aim was to express Jesus' town of origin. An interpreter must either assume, as is common, that Mark either didn't know the correct way to say "of Nazareth" or that he knew a way of saying it that is otherwise unknown. Both of these are possible, but the translation picks up a third, more interesting, possibility: the odd word might be a reference to the words of the prophet that promise that there will come a shoot (netzer) from the stump of Jesse.

8. It has long seemed to me, on the basis of the scene in which Peter walks (briefly) on water, that Matthew heard at least as much "sinks like a . . ." as he heard "solid as a . . ." in Peter's name.

9. Emmanuel Levinas, *Totality and Infinity*, 24.

10. Ibid., 202.

11. Ibid., 85.

12. A. E. J. Rawlinson, *St. Mark* (London: Methuen & Co., 1925), 99.

13. Lecoq, *Moving Body*, 139–40.

3. HOW TO MAKE MISTAKES

1. That means that the critiques of deconstructive reading are likely correct when they charge that deconstructive readings are parasitic upon the dominant, stable reading. That does not trouble us particularly, though we would be more likely to understand the relationship between the dominant and subversive readings not as parasitic, but as symbiotic. We would argue that these two interpretive moments, dominance and subversion, live together necessarily, and feed each other.

2. Found in J. A. Cramer, *Catenae Graecorum Patrum in Novum Testamentum* (Hildesheim, W. Germany: G. Olms, 1967).

3. Nils Dahl, "The Crucified Messiah," collected in *Jesus the Christ: The Historical Origins of Christological Doctrine,* ed. Donald Juel (Minneapolis: Fortress, 1991).

4. Viola Spolin, *Improvisation for the Theater* (Evanston, Ill.: Northwestern University Press, 1963), 81ff.

4. HOLDING TOGETHER/COMING APART

1. Aristotle, *Poetics*, 1450b, 27–31.

2. The reference is, of course, to Aristotle's *Poetics*.

3. Frank Kermode, *The Sense of an Ending: Studies in the Theory of Fiction* (London: Oxford University Press, 1967), 39.

4. Annie Dillard, *Living by Fiction* (New York: Harper & Row, 1982).

5. For example, see the volume of essays edited by Brian Swann, *Smoothing the Ground: Essays on Native American Oral Literature* (Berkeley: University of California Press, 1983), especially the essay by Kenneth Lincoln, "Native American Literatures," 3–38, and the essay by Kenneth M. Roemer, "Native American Oral Narratives: Context and Continuity," 39–56.

6. Leslie Marmon Silko, *Storyteller* (New York: Arcade, 1981). See also the volume of essays edited by Devon A. Mihesuah: *Indians and Academics: Researching and Writing about American Indians* (Lincoln: University of Nebraska, 1998), especially the essay by Angela Cavender Wilson, "Grandmother to Granddaughter: Generations of Oral History in a Dakota Family," 27–36.

7. Again I hear my grandfather, the carpenter. Structuralism always seemed to be an attempt to derive the Unified Building Code (UBC) of all existing narrative. The UBC specifies what can be done in building a house, given the materials that are available. A joist made of Douglas fir can span a distance of sixteen feet. A joist of spruce/pine spans only a distance of thirteen feet. The available materials make the determination. A certain number of nails are required for particular tasks. Again, experience and the characteristics of the available materials set the limits and open up the possibilities.

8. It is, of course, open to question whether it could even be meaningful to speak of "rejecting culture," but that is (after all) a central point being argued in this chapter.

9. One of the best sketches of this position, though not offered by a partisan to it, is found in Rebecca Chopp's *The Power to Speak: Feminism, Language, God* (New York: Crossroad, 1989).

10. For this argument, see Steiner's *Real Presences* (Chicago: University of Chicago Press, 1989). He makes a related argument much earlier, in *In Bluebeard's Castle* (New Haven, Conn.: Yale University Press, 1971). The development over the years is well worth examining.

11. For a thorough treatment of the sides of this fencing match, see any good handbook on literary criticism. Especially recommended is Bonnie Klomp Stevens and Larry L. Stewart, *A Guide to Literary Criticism and Research* (Fort Worth: Harcourt, Brace, Jovanovich, 1987). For a more detailed exploration, see Art Berman, *From the New Criticism to Deconstruction: The Reception of Structuralism and Post–Structuralism* (Urbana: University of Illinois Press, 1988).

12. See Aristotle's *Politics*.

13. For an exploration of what the matter of difference, difficulty, and irreducible multiplicity mean for theology and culture, see especially Kathryn Tanner's *Theories of Culture: A New Agenda for Theology* (Minneapolis: Fortress, 1997).

14. Tanner, *Theories*.

15. Eric D. Hirsch, *Validity in Interpretation* (New Haven: Yale University Press, 1967).

16. Brian Blount, *Cultural Interpretation: Reorienting New Testament Criticism* (Minneapolis: Fortress, 1995).

17. See, for reference, Bruno Bettelheim's discussion of this old story in his *The Uses of Enchantment: The Meaning and Importance of Fairy Tales* (New York: Vintage Books, 1977). For another angle on such stories, see Clarissa Estes Pinkola's *Women Who Run With the Wolves: Myths and Stories of the Wild Woman Archetype* (New York: Ballantine, 1992).

18. Contemporaries often seem impossibly far apart, as George Steiner notes when pointing out that Tennyson and Rimbaud were contemporaries.

19. James Thurber, *Fables for Our Times* (New York: Harper & Brothers, 1940).

BAD BOYS OF THE BIBLE
Exploring Men of Questionable Virtue
BARBARA J. ESSEX

In *Bad Boys of the Bible,* Essex reveals a side of seven well-known men of the Bible—Cain, Abraham, Adam, Samson, Lot, Jacob, and Jephthah—not usually reflected upon or even considered in most preaching and teaching. This informative book is written for the average layperson and includes reflection questions, suggestions for using this resource for preaching and teaching, and a bibliography for further study.

ISBN 0-8298-1466-3/Paper/144 pages
$14.00

BAD GIRLS OF THE BIBLE
Exploring Women of Questionable Virtue
BARBARA J. ESSEX

Designed as a 14-week study, *Bad Girls of the Bible* explores the Bible's accounts of traditionally misunderstood or despised women, including Lot's wife, Delilah, Jezebel, Salome, and Sapphira. The book challenges traditional, patriarchal perspectives and offers fresh interpretations while making biblical exegesis comprehensible to the average layperson.

ISBN 0-8298-1339-X/Paper/112 pages
$14.00

BODACIOUS WOMANIST WISDOM

LINDA H. HOLLIES

Hollies takes a look at the "bodaciousness" of women of color through stories of biblical women such as Queen Esther, Mary, the "bent over woman" in Luke 13, and other unnamed biblical women. She launches her discussion of this bodaciousness through the lens of womanist theology and discusses the journey of African American women who drew strength from their destitute state by weaving a quilt of resistance and resiliency.

ISBN 0-8298-1529-5/Paper/144 pages
$18.00

DAUGHTERS OF DIGNITY
African Women in the Bible and the Virtues of Black Womanhood

LAVERNE MCCAIN GILL

Daughters of Dignity seeks to explore the virtues of love, wisdom, justice, hope, and faith for African American women by tracing their historical, theological, and biblical contexts. Gill also provides new insights into these virtues as reflected in the stories of African women in the Bible such as Hagar, Zipporah, Rahab, and the Queen of Sheba, and paralleled with modern-day pioneers like Rosa Parks, Sojourner Truth, Mary McLeod Bethune, and Fannie Lou Hamer.

ISBN 0-8298-1373-X/Paper/144 pages
$17.00

ENCOUNTERS WITH THE EVER-PRESENT GOD

HOWARD W. ROBERTS

Roberts illustrates how biblical stories intersect with contemporary life by teaching readers to pray meaningfully and look at the lives of biblical characters who struggled with their faith. The book explores biblical accounts of how God came to those people and then builds bridges from the biblical lives to contemporary lives.

ISBN 0-8298-1435-3/Paper/144 pages
$12.00

JESUS AND THOSE BODACIOUS WOMEN
Life Lessons from One Sister to Another
LINDA H. HOLLIES

Linda Hollies serves up new spins on the stories of biblical women. From Eve to Mary Magdalene, portraits of the bodaciousness of the many matriarchs of the Christian tradition will prove to be blessings for readers. Study questions and examples of how one can grow in faith, spirituality, and courage—bodaciousness—are included at the end of each chapter.

ISBN 0-8298-1246-6/Paper/224 pages
$12.00

MOON UNDER HER FEET
Women of the Apocalypse
KIM S. VIDAL

Moon Under Her Feet is a guide to discovering and understanding the symbolic meanings of the female images in the Book of Revelation. Through examining characters such as Jezebel and the nameless female figure for which this book is entitled, *Moon Under Her Feet* aims to redefine what it means to be an empowered woman who achieves dignity based on equality, freedom of expression, self-empowerment, and solidarity with other women.

ISBN 0-8298-1415-9/Paper/128 pages
$10.00

VASHTI'S VICTORY
And Other Biblical Women Resisting Injustice
LAVERNE MCCAIN GILL

In *Vashti's Victory*, Gill examines and discusses six Bible stories of women who rebelled against oppression in order to have God's work made manifest in the world. Gill goes beyond the biblical narratives that direct attention to the primarily male leaders and instead focuses on a more holistic view of the story. The biblical women featured are compared to contemporary women. Study questions are included at the end of each chapter.

ISBN 0-8298-1521-X/Paper/128 pages
$16.00

To order these or any other books from The Pilgrim Press, call or write to:

THE PILGRIM PRESS
700 PROSPECT AVENUE
CLEVELAND, OH 44115-1100

Phone orders: 800·537·3394 (M–F, 8:30am–4:30pm ET)
Fax orders: 216·736·2206

Please include shipping charges of $4.00 for the first book and $ 0.75 for each additional book. Or order from our Web site at www.pilgrimpress.com.

Prices subject to change without notice.